THE POWER OF CHANGE IS WITHIN YOU!

Dedicated To You

Dear reader,

I promise you, from the beginning, that this book has the power to reorganize your whole way of thinking on how to apply the Universal Laws of Attraction, step by step!

I guarantee you that the transformational power of this book is simply amazing, and

YOU ....

hold in your hands, right now, a 100% practical tool by which to activate this power in your life.

Contents

Foreword — 9

Part I. THE GUARANTEE OF CHANGE
Leaf 0: Why is this book different? — 11
Leaf 1: The image of change seen from above — 15
Leaf 2: The importance of the spiritual component in the Concept of Attraction — 20
Leaf 3: The importance of the scientific component in the Concept of Attraction — 27

Part II. LAWS GOVERNING THE CONCEPT OF ATTRACTION AND THE TOOLS FOR THEIR PRACTICAL APPLICATION

Law 1: Law of Positive Thinking — 31
Law 2: Law of Consciousness — 62
Law 3: Law of Attraction — 79
Law 4: Law of Least Resistance — 106
Law 5: Law of Visualization — 116
Law 6: Law of Gratitude — 134
Law 7: Law of Forgiveness — 143

Law 8: Law of Giving	151
Law 9: Law of Void	156
Law 10: Law of the Organized Plan	161

Part III. HOW TO MINIMIZE THE PAYMENT OF YOUR SPIRITUAL BILLS

Section 1: Identify the spiritual messages	183
Section 2: Is the wall too high?	193

Bibliography	197
About the Author	199

FOREWORD

This book is structured in a professional, strikingly clear manner that will guide you step by step in reprogramming your mental settings, which will allow you to materialize your future, as you want it. The structure of this entire book is organized to provide you a progressive understanding as you approach its end.

You now have available a precise methodology for reprogramming your mind towards achievement of results. The functionality of concepts and strategies that you will discover is remarkably precise and for this reason, please remember that I am offering you exactly what I promise, and by the end of this book, you will be convinced that what I promised, I delivered!

The reality is that most sources of information regarding the Law of Attraction simplify the process of materialization so much, that if you apply those strategies (and perhaps you have), your chances of getting concrete results are low, for the following two reasons:

01. First reason: information is truncated, incomplete, overly simplified;

02. Second reason: you are not provided with a complete set of practical tools to apply in the materialization process.

In other words, you have to manage on your own! In these circumstances, you cannot correctly understand the Law of Attraction and therefore cannot apply it to your life to acquire what you want.

However, here the tone changes radically, since you're not alone anymore. I'll help you transfer into your life, step by step, all the knowledge that I make available to you through this book. You will find that just by reading this book, you'll probably venture into the most important mental journey of your life. If you apply the laws governing the Concept of Attraction, this process will correspond with the opening of a gate in your mind that you will not be able to close again, because you will gain a level of knowledge and energy that will not allow you to return to your old patterns of thinking.

Sincerely,

Gabriel Radu

PART I. THE GUARANTEE OF CHANGE

LEAF 0: WHY IS THIS BOOK DIFFERENT?

From the beginning, I want you to know that this book is completely different from everything you've encountered so far concerning the Law of Attraction. Not only will you radically change your vision about your mental potential, but you will program your future from both a spiritual and scientific perspective, using the most powerful tools in the process of change.

The Concept of Attraction, known by most as the Law of Attraction, enjoyed an increasingly growing international proliferation, through books, audio CDs, videos, articles, seminars, TV shows, coaching sessions, etc. Thus, there are enough information channels through which to access the mysteries of this concept, and if you've followed some of them, then I know that one of these two truths apply to you:

The first truth: In the best-case scenario, you have collected a lot of information from written, audio and video materials, and any courses you may have attended. The description of principles and laws was given to you using a cheerful attitude, then you were left high and dry with the information you only partially understood.

The second truth: The Law of Attraction was presented to you almost entirely from a spiritual perspective, but the reality is completely different, since the Concept of Attraction has two components: *a spiritual component and a scientific component.*

The spiritual component, no matter how well you apply it, simply is not enough. It is only half of the Concept of Attraction. How the Law of Attraction is presented in most sources of information sends the wrong idea that your life will change overnight if you add spiritual power to what you want and will take some action to this end. Let me tell you something: this is not true, nor will it be! This is the most common reason why most people try to apply the Law of Attraction, and then say "it does not work," "this is silly." However, I assure you that it works, and the results you get in your life are actually manifestations of how you understand and apply the law.

The real problem comes from the fact that most people do not understand the law, because it is generally presented to them only as an incomplete picture of how the materialization process should be applied. However, getting results is subject to the full knowledge and proper application of the laws that govern the Concept of Attraction.

Most people (perhaps this is your case?) led by the desire to penetrate the secrets of the concept of materialization, try to understand, forward and apply the techniques they learn, but realize the information they have is quite slippery, sometimes truncated, sometimes inaccurate and in many cases leaves much room for interpretation.

And then, you find yourself alone once again at the stage where you want to take action, but you do not have the tools to do so. It's like being sent to dig in the garden but with bare hands. You are just being told, "If you firmly believe that you will succeed, you will succeed".

Nevertheless, we both know this simply is not enough. If so, all you think you will achieve, will become reality. And I assure you this is false!

Here is an example: If you do not have a very good voice, you will never become a singer, no matter how much you work and no matter how great your faith is. You see, faith is very good and without it, you will not achieve the desired result, but this is not enough. You need other components too.

What you get in this book, is in fact the result of thousands of hours of work. Perhaps you wonder: "That long?" Yes, that long, as to get this book into a shape so clear, unique and applicable to your life, I have invested thousands of hours of work. The techniques you will encounter are not shallow techniques. They have been tested and will truly have real power in your life. So, what makes this book different from other information sources you have accessed so far? What makes it completely different? Here is the answer: the uniqueness and real power to change your life, which you will acquire through this book, is shown by three clear guidelines:

01. The components of the Concept of Attraction (we're talking here about ten universal laws that constitute the foundation of this concept).

02. Each of the ten laws has either a scientific or spiritual foundation; five of them are presented from a scientific perspective and the other five from a spiritual perspective.

03. The concrete and practical tool for implementing each of the ten laws, so as to integrate the Concept of attraction into your life once and for all.

This methodology not only allows you to understand correctly, completely and once and for all the Concept of Attraction, but also provides you with practical tools to achieve the desired results.

Now you own the perfect tool for the transition from what you are and what you have at the moment, to what is really your materialization potential. The changing power of this book is simply amazing, and you hold in your hands the tool to activate this power in your life and for that, I personally congratulate you!

LEAF 1: THE IMAGE OF CHANGE SEEN FROM ABOVE

Both, you and I, want this book to make a big difference in your life by thinking and acting in terms of results. This is why I decided to work with you in an open manner, and for this reason allow me to show you right now the correct image of what is to be discovered in this book. So, are you ready? Let's start!

As you already know, the Concept of Attraction only has real power through the application of both components in the materialization process, the spiritual component and the scientific component. If you only apply the spiritual component, you will become a dreamer, left high and dry. If you only apply the scientific component, you will not add energetic and spiritual power to what you want to manifest in the physical plane. Lack of spiritual power brakes the physical manifestation of what you want.

As a conclusion, if you do not integrate both components into materialization, either you will fail to materialize what you want, or you will, but for a short period of time. Therefore, manifesting the power of the Concept of Attraction in your life is, in fact, the result of integrating both the scientific and spiritual components into the materialization process. It is very certain, as certain as the fact that tomorrow clouds will appear in the sky, or that after the day follows the night. Okay, let's continue.

The two components, spiritual and scientific, are integrated into a set of ten universal laws, which, in fact, are the foundation of this concept of attraction. And, to give you a foreground image of this foundation, I now will reveal the influence of each of the ten laws on your life.

01. *Law of Positive Thinking* – helps to eliminate forever the most unproductive thinking patterns in your life and to reconfigure to the right direction of focusing your thoughts. This thinking reconfiguration strategy will shape your course of action and therefore your results in your life.

02. *Law of Consciousness* – helps you to replace the strongest negative beliefs of your mind that keep away from results, with a new set of positive beliefs that bring you into a state of mental power.

03. *Law of Attraction* – helps you to control, at a scientific level, the process by which you materialize events, people, opportunities, circumstances, virtually, everything that is manifesting in your life.

04. *Law of Least Resistance* – helps you to minimize your combat and resistance against the events of your life and thus to enter into a state of emotional control.

05. *Law of Visualization* – helps you to impregnate the mental screen of your subconscious with images corresponding to what you want to manifest in the physical plane.

06. *Law of Gratitude* – helps you to manifest yourself in life by feeling gratitude for what you are and what you have at the moment. This vibrational shift will create further conditions, which will attract more to you, for which you should be more grateful.

07. *Law of Forgiveness* – helps you release your past resentments, which will rebalance your energetic system. Thus, the energy starts to flow freely through your body and your mind will move from a locked state into a state of liberation.

08. *Law of Giving* – helps you to establish the flow of abundance that comes to you. You see, in order to get, you first need to offer correctly, same as, in order to reap you must first saw fertile ground.

09. *Law of Void* – helps to eliminate what is useless in your life (both inside and outside of you). This process creates a gap, a void, and what gravitates towards you, will settle in this void. When discarding what is useless in your life, you actually remove negative vibrations of things, events, and people from your past.

10. *Law of the Organized Plan* – all the other nine laws have one goal: to help you create every possible condition that would enable the energetic and spiritual forces underlying the processes of materialization. However, activation of these forces is not sufficient to achieve results. You have to take concrete action in this regard, such as a powerful strategy and action plan.

If the first part of each law shows you the spiritual and scientific explanations presented in a manner that will give you a deep understanding, well, in the second part, the focus is in a 100% practical direction. All knowledge that you acquired in the first part of each law, will be applied in the second part, through clear and practical tools, easy to apply, which will help you materialize what you want in your life. This is in fact the practical model that will lead you, step by step, in applying the Concept of Attraction in your life.

Each of the ten laws is like a piece of a puzzle, and you can see the full picture only when you understand and correctly apply each component. Without knowing and correctly applying these laws, it is as if you want to finish a picture puzzle, but you don't have all the pieces. You will not succeed and this is very clear. The ten laws are the engines of your life towards results. The better you integrate them into your life, the more their propulsion power amplifies. Before proceeding further, let's go on a trip to your future together.

If you live seventy years, this is equal to about 25,000 days of life, and then you go to another state, called death. Calculate by yourself, in your case, how many of the 25,000 days have already passed. Now take into account that in the last ten years of your life you will not have the power to make an obvious change in your life. This is true for most people.

"How many days do you have left to produce real change in your life?"

If you have the advantage of being young enough, you have more than 13,000 days left. This is what is important to understand: do not throw your time and life in the dump of history. Now you have a real chance to make a difference. Change your predominant thoughts and you will change your life. Understand that changing your life results is subject to changing your mind. You will not produce different results with the same mind, governed by the same mental programs and doing the same activities with which you are familiar.

The strategies and techniques which I have provided in this book are designed to help you understand the secrets of the materialization processes of what you want and to integrate them into your life. You must go through them step by step and in the end you will have such a strong image of the change, that you'll wish to take action starting even now.

I guarantee that if you apply the concepts and strategies I make available, your life will see changes that you don't even dare to dream of at the moment.

LEAF 2: THE IMPORTANCE OF THE SPIRITUAL COMPONENT IN THE CONCEPT OF ATTRACTION

For most people the concept of spirituality is reduced to a mixture of components, such as soul, spirit, sacred, holy, divine law, God, etc.; this mix has as a binding connection a state that people call faith.

Here is what must be clearly understood: spirituality does not mean religion. You can connect to spirituality through the Concept of Attraction, through various religions (there are more than 15 religions), etc. Many people connect to spirituality through religion, such as Christians, Roman Catholics, Protestants, Muslims, etc. This does not mean that one religion is better than another. Jesus has not completed His work on Earth imposing a religion, as a religion is just a manifestation of spirituality, a way, a tool by which you connect to spirituality.

Unfortunately, in general, religion has now become rather a manifestation of rituals in a certain sequence. However, this sequence of rituals does not connect you with spirituality. The connection to spirituality is conditioned by emotional power, faith attached to these rituals and not by the rituals themselves. You cannot show your love without attaching feeling. You can do many things that from the outside can be seen as manifestations of love, but if you do not attach emotion to these events, they have no real energetic and spiritual power.

The fact that you believe in a certain set of rules specific to a religious cult, does not make you more spiritual or less spiritual than another person who believes in a different set of rules specific to another religious cult. All those religious cultures are just tools through you relate to spirituality. Not the way itself connects you with spirituality, but the vibration in which you place yourself, the emotion attached, and your faith. Spiritual power is manifested through you. If no spiritual power leaves from you, you cannot create a relationship with the divine plane. The relationship with the divine plane leads to prosperity, but prosperity initially appears in your consciousness and you manifest it spiritually, then energetically and in the end physically. What is materialized physically is actually just the shadow of energetic and spiritual manifestation. To build this relationship with the divine plane you must clearly define three directions:

- *Direction 1:* What is the way you relate to the divine forces (Concept of Attraction, Yoga, Meditation, Qigong, various religions, etc.)?
  The way is not important, since God is not a religion. If so, then some people would be privileged over others in front of the deity.

- *Direction 2:* What is this relationship for you, specifically, what are the laws, beliefs that clearly define this relationship?
  You cannot follow a path if you do not understand its rules. Makes sense?

- *Direction 3:* What are you doing spiritually in this regard?
  It is essential to know that your soul food is not mainly determined by what you do, but by your vibration when you do it. If what you do does not fill your soul with gratitude, then you'd better give up, because you are putting yourself in a wrong relation to the divine plane, and this mistake will turn against you.
  Disagreement with divine laws brings stress and

mental dissatisfaction, illness and bodily suffering, and poverty in your life. At the opposite polarity of such disagreement with the divine laws are in fact the laws of prosperity, happiness and success. Laws of prosperity are based on spiritual principles as the spiritual principles elevate you and keep you in a high vibration frequency that aligns you with your goals. Without adding spiritual power to your actions, what you attract will not have the power to survive over time. You attract, and then you lose. The loss will occur in a month or ten years, but it is a rule, you will lose.

Develop the habit of attracting prosperity correctly. Remember what you'll read further: you are a slave to your habits! So choose habits that lead you to a state of permanent prosperity. Gather prosperity only outside of you and you will lose it. Gather prosperity in your mind and then you will attract prosperity outside you. The prosperity outside you will always follow the prosperity of your mind. True prosperity that you gather outside you on the long term will be closely related to the prosperity of your mind. Where your mind and heart are, there will be your energy and the things in your life. This focus enables the state of faith in you. The reality is that people generally do not believe in what they see, but rather they see what they choose to believe.

"People only see what they are prepared to see."
Ralph Waldo Emerson

Therefore, whatever your faith is, you must be congruent with it, as only this faith can help you reach energy levels that allow you to materialize physically what you want. I am not saying that one's faith is better than another's, but I am asking you:
"Do your beliefs help you keep fit or conversely, make you sick?"

"Do they help you get what you want, or not?"

Synthesized in a simple and clear form, spirituality relates to your mission of life. So, what is your mission, why do you make a shadow on earth?

To help you further clarify the vision, this is what I want to add: *"Spirit is the Life, Mind is the Builder and the Physical is the result of what mind has built. Spirit and Mind are invisible forces, Physical is visible."*[1]

Therefore, first is spirit, then soul, mind, and finally the physical body. Your goal is to know your own ideals – physical (we mean the body), mental (we mean the mind) and spiritual (we mean the soul). Thus, the human being has only three reasons to live *"body-mind-soul"*. Let's talk briefly about each component:

- *Component 1: Body*
  You use a body that is a physical transport vehicle. Being material, its existence is obvious and you do not question it.

- *Component 2: Mind (conscious and subconscious)*
  You use your mind to think. Coaching, NLP, psychology, psychotherapy, emotional intelligence, are branches of science that deal with the study of the human mind. Nowadays, the mind is relatively well understood. As you cannot deny the existence of body, you cannot deny the existence of mind. By only thinking, you are continuously producing effects mentally and then physically.

---

[1] Cayce, Edgar. *Soul and Spirit*, Adevar Divin Publishing House, Brașov, 2009, p.12

- *Component 3: Soul*
  An invisible, spiritual component that gives life to your body. Soul development takes place in the physical plane, since here, on Earth; you have free will and decide what kind of soul you develop: a good or a bad one. Therefore, soul development takes place here, on Earth, in the physical world and it's a divine component.

In conclusion, the three components, *"body-mind-soul"* are interconnected and together they form your human experience. What you have experienced in the past, you experience in the present and what you will experience in the future, is determined by these three components. They are the only components that form your human experience. So, in everything you do, whether you know it or not, you try to satisfy these three reasons to live, *"body-mind-soul"*:

- 01. The body needs food, clothing, care, sleep, relaxation, otherwise it will decay;
- 02. The mind needs intellectual food, otherwise it will decay;
- 03. The soul also needs spiritual food (you can call it soul food), otherwise it will decay.

Perhaps now you wonder:
"What is soul food?"
Well, it is what you do for God, Allah, Buddha, Universe, etc. It is not important what you call it. It is important to define clearly what this connection means, this relationship you have with the divine plane. Think hard about it! You need *"food"* for the body, mind and soul, as these three components are interconnected like a single mechanism. The suffering of one of these three components *"body-mind-soul"* leads to suffering of the others, and thus imbalance occurs in the physical, mental and spiritual plane.

Here is a concrete example:
People subconsciously destroy themselves mentally.
You're probably wondering:
"How is this happening?"

Here is the process: they seek many reasons to be upset, most of them imaginary, then they are fixating on them, amplifying the meaning of these problems in their lives. So, they enter into a closed loop in which their problems attract more problems until they reach the stage where their negative thoughts take control of their mind almost completely.

From morning till night they poison their minds with negative thoughts in all directions, passing thus into a paralyzed state of mind. Afterwards, this state of mind generates negative emotions that affect the physical body, and these manifestations unbalance the body's energetic system and its relationship with spirituality.

In conclusion, you hold a body, use a mind, have a soul and you are a spirit, and what moves the entire body-mind-soul assembly is in fact the spirit. I will use a very simple metaphor to make myself easily understood as I explain what spirit is: consider an aquarium filled with water in which there is a fish. If the fish is the life form (i.e. the body-mind-soul assembly), well, water where the fish is, means metaphorically the spirit. The fish exists like an entity as the body-mind-soul assembly, but its life continuity is ensured only if there is water in the aquarium, similarly as the continuity of your life is assured only by spirit.

Therefore, the spirit is the life force that manifests through you, it is what keeps you alive. Spirit is the manifestation of God through you. Spirit exists in everything. Your physical existence can only be achieved through spirit. You see, if the soul belongs only to humans, animals, birds, and virtually everything that is alive, well, spirit exists in everything, both in animate and inanimate things, and is eternal.

"Spirit is expressed through everything that is eternal in the consciousness of mind or matter."[2]

Before moving on, here are the most important conclusions:

01. Spirituality refers to your mission of life.

02. To build a relation with the divine plane you must clearly define three directions:

- What is the way you relate to the divine forces?
- What are the laws that clearly define this relationship?
- What are you doing to this end, what is the feed of your soul?

03. Man has three reasons for living: *body-mind-soul*. They together form the human experience. You own a body, use a mind, you have a soul and you are a spirit. The spirit moves the whole *mind-body-soul* assembly.

04. Your goal is to know your own ideals – physical (we mean the body), mental (we mean the mind) and spiritual (we mean the soul).

05. What is materialized in the physical plane is really just a shadow of the mental and spiritual manifestations.

06. The role of the spiritual component in the Concept of Attraction is to enable the energetic and spiritual forces that allow physical materialization of what you want.

---

[2]*ibidem*, p.1

LEAF 3: THE IMPORTANCE OF THE SCIENTIFIC COMPONENT OF THE CONCEPT OF ATTRACTION

You currently have exactly what you wished to have! I know that hearing this statement, most of you will say:

"Well, this cannot be true. I did not want these negative events that have happened to me." And I ask you:

"Do you know anyone who has set a goal to attract negative things?"

"Did you hear somebody saying that his/her dream is to become the biggest loser?"

Of course not! No one wants to attract negative things. Yet, these negative or seemingly negative things manifest in their lives.

The reality is that most of your life experiences have not been attracted consciously, but subconsciously. The majority of experiences were attracted by your subconscious mind. If what you just read were not true, that means you'd attract results only through your conscious thoughts. And then, everything that would manifest in your life, are only positive events, while the negative ones would stay far away from you.

However, the events that occur in your life are attracted by you, but subconsciously. Think carefully: no sane mind would want to attract adverse events. However, they manifest precisely because you have subconsciously attracted them with your predominant thoughts that govern your mind. There are no events, people, circumstances, opportunities to manifest in your life, without you having attracting them, as they are manifested only by the power of your mind.

The scientific component which describes five of the ten laws of the Concept of Attraction, helps you understand and integrate scientifically into your life, how you materialize events, people, circumstances, opportunities. You can open your mind to such a way of thinking or you can refuse it totally. Life is about making choices. You can choose to be a victim, or whatever you like to be. But every choice has its price, and you are solely responsible for your actions and results in your life. Success has a recipe, just as failure has one. Success is the result of transfer into the physical plane of laws that govern success, just as failure is the result of violating the laws that govern success.

This book helps you organize your thinking, not only from a spiritual perspective but also from a scientific perspective, so the focus of your attention is directed towards what you really want.

The scientific component of the Concept of Attraction results in organizing your thinking to a high level of knowledge that will allow you to take control of your future once and for all. I do not know if you really realize, but now you hold in your hands a book that you will help you gain the power to change your own reality, by reconfiguring your mental settings. This reconfiguration is basically a way to strategically manage your predominant thinking and emotional energy. It's like assembling a machine. Each component must be set in place for the machine to work.

Your case is similar: predominant thinking and emotional energy must be strategically channeled, targeted, and focused towards what you really want. Do not fool yourself! Without going through the process of organizing your thoughts, the other techniques that you try to use to achieve results are just stories, they do not have force. I'm not saying they are not good. They are good as tools themselves, but their applicability greatly decreases if your mind does not initially go through a process of organizing your thoughts, based on the universal laws that govern prosperity, happiness and success. The change that you will make following the techniques I make available to you, will be permanent.

PART II. LAWS GOVERNING THE CONCEPT OF ATTRACTION AND THE TOOLS FOR THEIR PRACTICAL APPLICATION

LAW 1: LAW OF POSITIVE THINKING

PART 1: SCIENTIFIC DESCRIPTION OF THE LAW

Here is what this law states:
In life, in the long-term, you become exactly what you predominantly think, as the focus of your thoughts shapes your course of action and therefore dictates your results. Thus, what you are now is the result of your predominant thoughts and actions of the past. What you will be in the future will be the result of your predominant thoughts and actions today. In this context, we do not refer to occasional thoughts and actions, because they do not have a significant influence on the direction of action in your life, and therefore do not have actual power over your life's results. We are talking about your predominant thoughts and actions that you perform constantly, day after day, month after month, year after year.

Next, let's direct our attention to the mental function called thinking. Here is the truth: most people do not think! In the first phase, most will resist this categorical statement. I hope you are different, so let me tell you the truth! The reason that most resist is because their minds still do not properly understand the notion of thinking. For them, to think is to conduct a mental activity! However, the difference between the two processes is enormous. Mental activity is not the same thing as thinking, it is only accessing a database of an informational source in their brains. Mental activity is to access a mental function called memory. These people project again and again on their mental screen the same images, thoughts, beliefs, and emotions relating to events in their past. But this process is not thinking. Remembrances from the past form what is called memory. Further, the memory determines your perception of the reality of your past, which in turn affects your present reality.

Let's explore further why most people project on their mental screen the same images, again and again. Psychology and NLP are very clear in this respect: people have formed about 80% of their beliefs underlying their actions in life by the age of seven. Can these beliefs be changed? Absolutely! But the truth is that mental changes that most people make are so small that they have no real power to change the results.

Basically, they just re-access the same old beliefs planted in their minds when they were very young, then based on those beliefs, they make decisions and move to action. This means that their present actions are influenced by beliefs they have acquired since early age. Their brains are like computers on which several programs were installed. What these people do is re-access the same information again and again in different contexts of life. But this process is not thinking as thinking involves changing those mental programs installed since an early age. Therefore, not accidentally the motivational speaker and author Dr. Kenneth McFarland said: *"2% of the people think, 3% of the people think they think and 95% of the people would rather die than think."*

There are two pitfalls that can keep you trapped in the category of those who do not think. Be very careful, because it is simply amazing how easily you can fall in them:

Trap 1: To follow what people around you are doing.

The majority follows what people around them do. In most cases, they are guided by the opinions of others instead of their own thoughts. What happens outside, in the exterior, controls what happens inside their minds. The influence of others becomes stronger than their own thoughts. But remember: if you follow what most people do, you'll achieve the same results as the majority!

Trap 2: To live your life in the past.

Most people consume their time, which is the most important value, mentally and emotionally re-living past events, and in most cases, negative events from the past. But remember: if you live in the past, you will achieve now the same results as in the past!

If you have slipped into these traps, they will keep you trapped in the category of those who do not think. This type of mental activity, which we can call the lack of thought, will keep you in the past. The mental process is simple: you unload in the present all your emotional baggage from the past, talking about the past, living in the past emotionally, and identifying yourself by what you have been in the past. But this is about regressing, and you will feel strongly this regression somewhere in your future, when problems will start coming, so many and so quickly, that they will put you down. And then you'll say life is unfair. But it is exactly as you created it by your predominant thoughts and actions. You basically create your own reality by the way you think most of the time.

The psychological truth is that if you unload the past into the present, it actually materializes in the future, because what you are today is the result of the predominant thoughts and actions of the past. What you will be in the future is the result of the predominant thoughts and actions today. When you unload the past in the present, you actually self-program subconsciously to materialize in the future the same set of results as in the past. However, the future can only be materialized through the power of the present. Therefore, if you do not live in the present, you actually live in the past. So, do not think about what was, as you cannot change the future with yesterday's thoughts. The real cause of failure is just in your mind and is dictated by the way you predominantly think.

To give you a more complete view on the state of mind of living in the past, let's go for a car ride. Imagine that you are driving. While driving a car, to ensure your safety, you have to look forward and occasionally throw a glance in the rearview mirror to see what is happening behind the car. Now imagine that while driving your car you just look in the rearview mirror. What do you think will happen? It's pretty obvious where you'll be after 30 or 50 meters. Even if you are a professional driver, if you only look in the mirror to what is happening in the back, you will not know what is happening in the front and soon your car will be damaged. It is so in your case: if you look too much in the past, you will not have a future.

So think carefully what is the predominant thinking direction of your mind, because that is exactly the direction you're headed in the future. If you do not like it, then start right now to work on changing direction. Where others have succeeded, it means that you can succeed as well.

From a psychological point of view, what can be put into a mind, can be placed in almost any other mind. Therefore, you have a potential of which you are probably not even aware, because you have not really explored it. Your potential is connected to the outcome of your life only to the extent that you use it.

If until now we discussed the state of mind that we called the lack of thought, let's now set the spotlight on the mental state located in the opposite polarity. So:

"What is thinking and how to obtain positive thinking, focused on results?"
Stay close, because I will detail this topic for you right within this law.

Before going further, it is essential to note two important aspects of this law:

01. In life, in the long-term, you get exactly what you predominantly think, as the focus of your thoughts shapes the course of action and therefore dictates your results.

02. Mental activity is not thinking.

Okay, let's continue. Here is a powerful idea: whether you want to or not, whether you like or not, you generate thoughts continuously. You cannot stop this process. Research demonstrates that the common person has up to sixty thousand thoughts per day, but most are repeated from day to day: to go to work, I have to pay the bills, I have to go for shopping, toothpaste is over, I have to do cleaning, etc.

So thoughts cannot be stopped. It is applicable to you, to me and to everyone in a state called life. For most people, daily thoughts are like a grenade exploding with splinters flying in hundreds of directions. Same with thoughts: they are oriented in hundreds of directions, have no clear focus on specific objects, and produce extended changes in the long term.

So what you cannot do with your thoughts is stop them, but what you can do is target and refocus them towards specific and large-scale objects. Focused long-term thinking will change your life. Will the change occur overnight? Of course not! It is a process of changing that can take even years. But here is what I know: only those things for which you are willing to work with more consciousness, have value in your life. I guarantee to you: the focus in one part of your life will, over a period of several years, generate a change that at this time you don't even dare dream of. The idea of focusing on a single component of your life is an amazing idea. No matter how hard you work, until you don't go through predominant states of focus, you will fail to produce results far above the average. Thinking scattered in all directions has no power to change.

If I were to listen just 15 minutes how you talk about your life, I could say with accuracy if in the next 5 years you will live as a poor or a rich person. I want you to understand me from the proper perspective: I am not clairvoyant to read your future. I can only envisage from a proper scientific perspective how your thoughts materialize in your life. It is scientific knowledge.

Through this book, I wanted to offer you a large part of this knowledge that I have and that will help to produce a really big change in your life. I have provided you with principles and strategies that I have gathered during thousands of hours of work. Now you own them in a very well organized manner easy to understand and apply. The value you get through this book is colossal and you will see for yourself.

You know what? It does not cost you more to think big, but the costs will be huge if you do not! Price of your ignorance of your own thinking is your life itself. If you do not give clear direction to your thinking, focused on goals, the world around you will give it a direction. And so, you will think like them, you will act like them, you will get about the same results as them, you will live among them, and you will be like them. And now, I will tell you something that might hurt you: you like being between them. Are you wondering how I know? Simple! If it were not so, then you would be in the process of change, and when you are in the process of change you do not identify with their way of thinking, because it feels like drinking poison. Now that you understand, you can open your mind to a different pattern of thought and action that will push you towards results.

Until you really get control of your thoughts, the outside world is what controls your way of thinking. Over 90% of people are mentally programmed to let the outside world control them, and influence their radical decisions. You can see this in their professional life, personal life, in their social relations. Simply, these people wait to be guided from the outside and easily follow the views of others. They take advice from others, integrate them into their minds and then believe they belong and identify with them, and then move on to action. But this advice does not come from themselves. It was taken from the outside, from people who simply go through life at random. Do you know what most people have in mind? Much confusion and many opinions.

Here is a strong idea for you and I recommend that you integrate it well into your mind:
Don't you dare think that by using the minds of the majority you will achieve great things. This is not going to happen ever.

Let us focus our attention once again on this idea: you cannot achieve great things, using the minds of the majority.

And now, let me ask you:
"Whom do you follow in life, those who have a focused mind, a positive attitude, a mindset of continuous growth or those with minds full of opinions?"
Give yourself an answer.

Let me help you as much as possible because that's what I really wanted. Before moving on, I dare you to do the following exercise: Take a pen and a sheet of paper and write the 6 people in your life with whom you spend most of your time. Stop reading right now and write the 6 people in your life with whom you spend most of your time. Now analyze the results achieved in life by each one of them.

Be prepared for this is the interesting part: in five years, you will be at their average level, as *Jim Roth* in *The law of averages* demonstrated. You're probably wondering: How will this happen?

Here is the process: the psychological reason for which you become the average of people that you spend most of the time with, is because between you and them there is a constant transfer of attitudes and information, which it will further cause the beliefs and actions you'll do. Your results in life are directly proportional to the beliefs that govern your mind. Therefore, if you do not like what you have discovered, start looking for ways to change the average of the persons with whom you spend most of your time.

If you do not find new people to replace those who pull you down, then I'll give you the solution: replace them with people on CDs, from books, i.e. those who talk about principles of materialization, about attitude, leadership, dreams, decision power, communication, emotional intelligence, the principle of success, etc. Make this change and it will make a big difference. Put your headphones in your ears and listen to those people on the street, on the train, in the subway, while shopping, and even when you clean the house. Maximize your time spent on the results of your life. That I guarantee is a great idea that will produce a significant change in your life. Success feeds from powerful positive thinking, focused on clearly defined objectives, just as failure feeds from disorganized thinking. Success does not mean to get to the top. Success is dictated by how high you bounce when you get to the ground. Now we come together to the phase when we can state the third important aspect of this law:

03. You cannot stop your thoughts, but you can direct them to specific objectives to make a big difference in the results of your life, and for that, connect with the right people.

It is a universal truth that success depends on the way you think, just as failure does. In other words, how you predominantly manage your thinking leads you in one direction or another. William James has focused this truth in a very suggestive phrase. Here it is: *"We are where we are and we are what we are because of the predominant thoughts that occupy our minds."* We should once again partake of this truth: *"We are where we are and we are what we are because of the predominant thoughts that occupy our minds."* Told in a very simple form, your results depend on your thoughts.

And now comes the question for you:
"Has someone taught you how to think?"
I know it is possible this question is going to sound weird.

You're probably wondering:
"What do you mean by someone teaching me how to think?"
Well if no one taught you how to think, what makes you think that you really think? What makes you think that what happens in your mind can be called thinking and not mental activity? That should make you think a lot!

Here is a powerful truth: your thoughts are what kills or builds you. Lack of thought is the biggest disease in the world. Over 90% of people are suffering from this disease. Remember what Dr. Kenneth McFarland said: *"2% of the people think, 3% of the people think they think, and 95% of the people would rather die than think."*

Seriously, do you want to convince yourself of that? I challenge you: listen to the conversations of most people wherever you are (on the street, on the bus, shopping, at the bank, even when walking). Simply, just listen to what people are saying. Here is what you'll discover: most people talk about shortages, life dissatisfaction, criticism, insignificant things, injustice, bad times, or little money.

By the words they use, these people unload to those around them, the thoughts that predominantly govern their minds. Their minds are ruled by poverty consciousness; they have developed a poverty mentality and therefore will attract poverty in their personal and professional life, in relationships, in almost all aspects of their lives, because this is their consciousness.

Let us look at rich people's minds. They have a completely different mentality. They have the mentality of abundance, prosperity, success, and growth. Why? Simple! Because they predominantly think and act in this direction, day after day, month after month, year after year. Don't be fooled, their success is no accident. Success is a result.

Practically, both, the poor and the rich use their minds, but the focus of their thoughts is in opposite polarities. Sure, the following question comes naturally:
"What causes the difference between the two mental patterns of thought?"
Here is the answer: while some have discovered how to direct their thoughts and energy towards what really produces long-term results, the others have no idea what happens in life and go at random, leaving themselves be guided by the opinions of others. Thoughts of others have taken over their minds, and they do not even know it.

Now think specifically in your case:
How much do you let yourself be influenced by the thinking of ordinary people?
Give yourself an answer – (otherwise you poison your mind with delusions).
Referring to the two directions of thought, situated in opposite polarities, this is what I want to say:
"It is not important where you are!"

"It is not important what happened to you until now!"

"The circumstances where you are now are not really important, because you're not created by the circumstances, circumstances are created by you!"

"It is not important what is your financial situation today!"

"It is not important what people you are among now!"

All these reasons do not have any real power unless you give them power over how you think about them. What really matters is that your future always starts with the present. Think well: those who have reached success now, once had a beginning and left in their process of development from levels which in most cases were far below yours. They succeeded because they have put their thoughts in order and reprogrammed their mental computer towards success. You have to start from here if you want to reach success.

On the other hand, the ordinary person has a completely different mindset, has a disorganized way of thinking and practically, his/her physical, emotional and intellectual energies are not directed or channeled towards a specific purpose. This mode of mental operation unbalances the ordinary person, keeps him/her handcuffed into the trap of disorganized thinking, random thinking and blocks his/her brain into a mental state called lack of thought.

I know it is not easy to change your dominant mind set. If it were easy, everyone would do it. But here is what I know: for that who doesn't make this mental change, nor the retirement, nor work tomorrow, nor the life of quiet desperation, nor the poverty will be easy. So what price do you pay for change, what are you doing about it? Give yourself an answer – (otherwise you fight against your success).

There are two types of mentality in the world:

01. mentality of stagnation (this category includes those who are constantly trying to keep what they have and work day after day in this direction). Their common thinking revolves around the following idea: to be at least how it was, to get what they got so far, to be the same.

02. mentality of growth (this category includes those who constantly pursue continuous growth, day after day, month after month, year after year). They aim to achieve increasingly high levels.

And now here's the question for you:
"Do you belong to those with a mentality of stagnation or growth?"
Do not be ignorant about your future, so give yourself the answer before moving on. Here is the thinking of most people: they do not pay conscious attention to their thoughts. Simply, they pay attention to all thoughts going through their mind, whatever their nature is. They are not selective, they think at random. But from the moment you put your mind in order, you'll go into a state of mental awakening, because your thoughts are mental programs that are formed after your own reality.

Only by thinking and then moving to action, you are continuously producing effects in the physical plane. If you were not producing effects by thinking, then you are in a completely different state called death! When you become aware of the materialization power of your thoughts, you automatically realize that, in fact, you are the creator of your own reality by the way you predominantly think.

The materialization of your thoughts on the physical plane is not instantaneous, and that's good. It manifests later in the physical plane, usually within a few months or years. But that's good, because otherwise you would have the power of instant materialization. Think and immediately materialize.

- Think positive, instantly materialize positive.
- Think negative, instantly materialize negative.

Transpose yourself, mentally and emotionally, in the following thinking hypothesis:

- If you would have even now the power to materialize instantly, how fast would you change your focusing direction of thoughts from negative to positive? Will you have the courage to think negatively?

The materialization process is quite similar to the process by which a flower grows. First, you put the seed in fertile ground. Then, make sure to wet it frequently, have patience for it to grow and somewhere in the future you will have a flower. Thinking is similar: Place a positive thought in fertile ground (whereas if you have a hundred negative thoughts in addition to the positive one, the negative thoughts will swallow it). Then you power that thought daily, bringing it on the mental display, adding emotional load to this process, doing daily work in this direction, and somewhere in the future, your thought will materialize.

I offer you these mental representations of remarkable simplicity, just to simplify the complicated things about understanding the process of materialization. Only in this way, you will acquire correct knowledge that will lead you towards the results you want.

People who have decided to change their thinking simply no longer watch TV, do not read newspapers or negative information on the Internet, and no longer connect with negative people. They basically disconnect from any source of negative information so that they greatly minimize the external environmental influence on them.

At the same time, they:

- direct their thinking to what they want to achieve in their lives;
- connect with positive people;
- read motivational books;
- listen to CDs with successful strategies;
- build their action plans for the next years;
- follow daily subconscious changing programs;
- apply principles and strategies for success in their lives.

So what do you think is the consequence of the process of positive focus? The answer is obvious: while negative thinking, from lack of food, becomes increasingly less, positive thinking becomes increasingly larger. The more attention you give to something, whether positive or negative, the more you increase your thought-related energy in that direction and the likelihood of attracting it into your life becomes increasingly larger.

So, success is no accident. Success is a continuous process of mental reprogramming and smart work towards results. All wise people of the world argued a great truth by various forms of content: thinking is the most important value that you have, as it represents the shutter of all your actions and therefore the results of your life. These simple truths are only elements of simple psychological principles.

Now I think you have come to the understanding level where we can formulate the fourth important aspect of this law:

04. Even as of today you can begin to act mentally, emotionally and physically in the direction of change, no matter what the conditions of your life are at the moment.

Are you ready now to venture forth?

- If your answer is positive, I'll help you organize your thoughts, and for that I make available to you, right now, a powerful tool with 100% practical applicability, easy to apply but yielding a great deal of changes in your life;

- If your answer is no, then throw the book out the window right now, and someone will find it and apply with great awareness the techniques and strategies inside the book and will change his/her life.

Next, I will provide a practical tool with a great power of transformation to change your thoughts. So, are you ready to discover? I shall call this tool: Unproductive Thinking Patterns.

These thinking patterns keep you handcuffed into the failure traps, away from results. The reason for which I present them is just to make you aware of them so that you do not fall into the trap of sick and unproductive thinking that moves you away from results. See that polar opposite of this idea is true: only when you know how to avoid these unproductive thinking patterns, you will approach the results, since what is outside these unproductive thinking patterns is actually positive thinking! I guarantee: the reason for which you have not yet achieved the desired results, will be identified in at least one of these thinking patterns.

Pattern 1: Negative Thinking

First, I give you a very significant example in this respect. Here is the story:

"Once upon a time there was a race of frogs. Their goal was to reach the top of a high tower. Many people gathered to see the race and support the frogs. The race was scheduled to begin. In reality, no one in the crowd ever thought that the frog will reach the top of that tower. All one could hear were exclamations like:
"Ohhh, what weariness. They will never be able to reach the top!"
"They cannot succeed. The tower is too high!"
The frogs began to abandon, except for one that was briskly climbing on. The crowd continued to yell:
"It's too tiring! None will be able to reach the top."

More and more frogs admitted defeat and abandoned the race. Only one continued to climb. It did not want in any way to abandon it. At the end, all the frogs renounced, except for one frog that, with enormous ambition and strength, managed to reach the top of the tower. Finally, all the other frogs and audience wanted to know how the frog managed to reach the top, when all the other frogs were forced to abandon the race. The winning little frog was deaf."[3]

---
[3]Unknown author, *Frog allegory*

Moral of the story: never listen to people who have a bad habit of being negative, as they will destroy your most beautiful wishes and hopes you carry in your soul. Instead, become aware of the power of your thoughts, for everything you think affects what you do. Above all, just be deaf when someone tells you that your dreams cannot become reality.

Remember: if your thoughts will follow the circumstances in your life, then your long-term results will be very low. If you let others control your mind, you will have a miserable life. You must have control of your thoughts as thoughts today are the habits of tomorrow and habits will determine your results.

Listen carefully what I want to tell you, be present with me, as the action is happening here. What I will say is an idea that will clear your vision on how to attract the results in your life.

Here is the idea:

- Rich people think of wealth.
- Poor people think of poverty.
- Sick people think of disease.
- Believers think of faith.

And talk about it! They put this emotional load in it and therefore they get it.

What happens basically? Each one reaps in life exactly what governs predominantly their mind. The same goes for you and me. Negative thinking will keep you away from results. You will never be able to get positive results in the long term, having a mind governed by negative thinking. And I am sure, you will not encounter any person for which the following idea works:

"I remain at my negative thinking and I continue in this way until I become rich or successful. This is never going to happen."

We both know that the mind needs intellectual food, otherwise decays. So allow me to offer your daily menu. Open it mentally and you will find the menu contains two strange questions, and at the bottom of the menu, you will find written your name and your signature. That means it is yours! So let's start. Are you ready?

The first strange question:
"Aren't you sick of thinking the same thoughts every day?"
Give yourself the answer now!

The second strange question:
"Aren't you tired of doing day after day, the same things that bring dissatisfaction and frustration towards your own life?
Give yourself the answer now!

And if you're not much different from most people, you'll probably say:
"But what else to do, because I cannot and I do not know how to do anything else. I would like to do it differently, but I cannot!"
I have a secret and I admit it is actually funny for me to reveal it to you. Here is the secret: turn the page on the menu and you'll see that the first two questions were just for the mental process heating. Now the tough questions come out.

The first tough question for you:
"When did you decide that? When did you decide that you cannot?"
Give yourself an answer now, otherwise, the question will explode somewhere in your future and I guarantee

that you will be the one to suffer the consequences! You cannot run from what is in you, you can only delay it, but you will suffer the consequences with added interest. So: When did you decide that? When did you decide that you cannot?

The second tough question for you:
"How long from today will you decide to embrace this blind belief: I cannot?"

Give yourself the answer now if you do not want to pay the price later with added interest. And if you did answer this question, you can close the menu and move forward. Thanks for your involvement !

We continue with a harsh reality: integrate into your life the belief *"I cannot"*, until you reach the time when you do not have enough life to produce change. You can integrate this belief in your life, you can even let it haunt your mind. Hold tight to this belief because it is yours. Nobody wants to steal it from you, because no one wants to have a miserable life. So if your decision is *"I cannot"*, then stay with this belief and let dissatisfaction and frustration to pile up and make their place in your life.

We both know the truth: your thought is creator, you hold the power to create your own life, so stick to what you believe, continue to think the thoughts of yesterday, and this will bring more dissatisfaction, frustration and hopelessness, because you go deeper into the emotional memories of your past. But this has nothing to do with creating something new, that's just about your past. If you expect a different life, thinking as in the past and doing the same things as before, well, that does not make sense!

In general, people have a negative thinking, as they predominantly think about what they do not want. To convince yourself of this, I recommend you to do the following exercise: for a few days test as many people as possible with a very simple technique that I propose below. Here is what to do: listen to the words of people. Wherever you go, just listen to what people are saying. In most cases, you'll find that they talk about events that they did not want, they talk about negative and set the emotional load in this process. So, listen to their words, and when you are engaged in discussion with them, tell them the following:

"I am interested to hear anything you have to say, provided it is positive."

You will have a big surprise. Most will remain speechless. I challenge you, do it, because it is a practical exercise of awareness of the influences that the surrounding people have on your way of thinking. You must become very selective with the people around you as you become the average of people with whom you spend most of the time. Think very well about it.

Imagine that all negative aspects of your life were a complex mechanism with gears. When you think negatively, you put in motion some gear which turns another gear, and if you continue for years to pay attention to negative things, you will engage the whole mechanism, which will run at a dizzying rate. The more you think about negativity, the more you feed this complex system with energy, so it will run at increasingly higher rate; bad things will come to you increasingly more and faster. This fight will make your life a nightmare and instead of living your dream, you will live your nightmare.

Negative thoughts and emotions exist in your mind as you pay attention to them. Without your attention, they become smaller and smaller until they no longer have power and then your mind stops seeing them, because they are no longer there. They were replaced with positive thoughts and emotions. So change your emotional attention and actions to the things you want. Do not pay attention to what you do not want and what is negative. Not to pay attention to negative thoughts, means not to listen, talk and think negatively.

Change your focus towards positive thoughts: listen, speak and think only in the direction of what you want. Negativity cannot be defeated thinking to it or fighting against it. Negativity can be defeated only with positivity. If you want to overcome evil, connect with good.

Pattern 2: Devalued Thinking

Devalued Thinking means to deliberately consider you inferior to others. This damaging mode of thinking throws you down permanently, because mentally you consider yourself inferior to others whom you think they are better, smarter, and wiser than you.

A highly entertaining movie runs on the mental screen of persons who fall into the trap of devalued thinking. Here is the mental movie: every time you fall into the trap of devalued thinking, in your mind you are convinced that others around you are better, smarter, and wiser than you. On the other hand, others think the same as you: that others are better, smarter, and wiser. It is as if you scare each other. If you take seriously the question I address below, it will shake your consciousness a little. So, here is the question: What kind of image of yourself have you built? Is it strong, positive or one that pulls you down day after day?

Here's what is essential to understand: if you fall into the trap of devalued thinking, you are the one who deliberately puts yourself in inferiority. No one else puts you in inferiority. You put yourself in inferiority. However, if someone manages to make you inferior, it is because your attitude allows this, it is because your picture of yourself lacks the attitude and confidence, and is devalued. In other words, your presence has no verticality to others; your presence does not send a positive attitude.

Where can you see the manifestation of this thinking pattern? Generally everywhere, but here are some specific situations with which you are probably more familiar:

- personal life (you place yourself in inferiority to your partner and generally agree with everything he/she says);

- professional life (you think others are better and thus you are trying to please them, so that you are accepted in their team);

- interview (you think you are small and worthless, and the employer is like an eagle who spreads its wings to shatter you);

- in relationships (you generally recognize easily those with devalued thinking, as they try to agree with everyone).

Here is the painful truth: until you permanently cure yourself of this pattern of thinking, but absolutely permanently, you will be pulled down.

"The key to every man is his thought."
Ralph Waldo Emerson

So, I ask you again:

"What picture of yourself do you want to build? When you look in the mirror, what are you saying to yourself? Do you have force? Do you have verticality? Do you have a good attitude? Do you see a strong image?" Think very carefully about it!

Pattern 3: Unfocused Thinking

It is specific to those involved in all sorts of activities at random! For them, anything which appears in their way represents an opportunity and jump to take it! These people are involved in all sorts of activities at random and do not follow a strategic plan that would result in a clear direction towards a long-term result.

You know what is really painful?
Although they are aware their actions do not lead to results that make them happy in the future, they continue to do those things day after day. Imagine what it would be to get to the end of life with pain in your heart and shattered dreams, realizing that you went through life randomly, and you let those who do not have dreams destroy your dreams, to pull you down constantly.

So, unfocused thinking does not produce results. If you really want results, this involves strong mental clarity; specifically, you need to know the following:

"What is your objective?" (Think about it: if you do not even know the goal, how can you achieve it?)
"Why is it important for you?"
"What results do you want to achieve?"
"What is your action plan to achieve that goal?"

These four questions are fundamental in achieving results. Without this mental clarification, you do not reach concrete results in life, you just walk. Maybe you will not get everything you had planned, but certainly, you will not get what you did not even propose! Be careful which way you choose to go in life, as most places have road signs that say the word *"NOWHERE"*. You decide which signs to place on your life highway: those that read *"NOWHERE"* or those that read *"YOUR DREAMS"*?

Pattern 4: Small Thinking

You cannot achieve great things with small thinking, having low expectations of yourself. Great things can be achieved only with great expectations. In other words, if you think small scale, do not expect to achieve great results. As you can see, the process of change begins in your mind; it takes place from the inside out and never vice versa.

"Why do you think most people fall into the trap of small thinking?"

Pay attention to their mental process when they set goals: they look at their past achievements, look at their skills now and then set a goal for the future.

Here is the trap: when you set a goal in this manner, you limit your future based on what happened in the past, depending on your past results. I mean you want to get different results, you want to be the best, you want to become somebody, you want to have influence, but what you do is that you relate to what you were before. If you act in this manner, you take little distance from your way of thinking in the past and therefore of your past results. If you want great results, you must have a high-level thinking. So, do you think people who have a hundred times more than others, work a hundred times more? No!

Of course they don't. Good, but what do they do differently? Well, they think on a scale of one hundred fold. In conclusion, you cannot achieve great things with the mind governed by small thinking. Unfortunately, there are still many people living governed by small thinking. And that brings them now and will bring in the future very little results. People who think in the short term have no courage to act in the long term, because their minds are not scheduled in this regard.

My goal is to help you really want to get into a state of awakening your consciousness, to become self-responsible, to take action in terms of objectives and long-term tangible results. And I will do for you exactly what I say.

Pattern 5: Accusatory Thinking

The world is full of accusers that blame others for the results they obtain. This is the reality, this is why I recommend to you immunize yourself against this way of thinking with the Daily Positive Dose.

Let me tell you how the minds of accusers work: in their consciousness, everyone is guilty for the lack of results that govern their lives. The culprit is the mayor, the boss, the president, neighbors; everyone is guilty for their results, but them.

If you think that others are guilty for your results, I have a strong question for you:

"Who makes the decisions for you?"
"Who forces you to listen to negative information?"
"Who forces you to do the same things you're used to?"
"Who forces you to work hard for little money?"

I'll give you the answer: you do it and do it deliberately. You take your own decisions in life. Therefore, you are primarily responsible for your results. If you like the results you have got and think you're headed in the right direction in the long term, I congratulate you. If you do not like the results, I encourage you to take continuous action on a large scale towards a well-determined objective to make a change.

These are the most unproductive thought patterns.
Now I want to paint you the big picture: the five patterns of thinking that we discussed, keep you handcuffed in the trap of failures, as you develop a closed, restricted, and limited mind.
What is outside the five patterns of thinking?
You probably guessed: Positive Thinking!

In other words, if you learn how to avoid the five unproductive thought patterns, you will automatically develop a positive thinking, focused on results. Now you have a powerful tool for verification of your way of thinking which helps you:

- avoid pitfalls in the process of thinking;
- make mental adjustments appropriate for positive thinking.

However, your goal is not to be focused on the five unproductive thought patterns, as the focus of your mind should actually be oriented in a positive direction. They represent only a verification tool. The only functional pattern of thought to know success, prosperity, happiness is the positive thinking. The tool that I have provided you by the five unproductive thought patterns has the power to re-organize your whole way of thinking in a way that focuses on results. Now pay attention to what I am about to say: no matter how much you work, until you develop a thinking focused on concrete results, you will slow down the appearance of physical results from your mental plane.

PART 2: PRACTICAL TOOL FOR LAW APPLICATION

We could call this tool the radiography of your thinking. If until now you have acquired a high level of knowledge about the scientific part of law, now the stress test follows! I recommend that you do it if you want to discover how you can increase results in your life. The test must be administered with great consciousness, honesty and responsibility. You may need a few hours, maybe more. If you want to do the test in five minutes, then it will really have no effect. Under these conditions, forget about the test, as it is not for you. Bury it in your consciousness, place a tombstone and continue to live the same life as before.

So, whatever your decision is, here is what to do:

- if the results in your life are not important, then you should not take the test;

- if the results in your life are important, then taking the test is a must.

The decision is yours. You decide whether it is important or not for your life! I only offer you alternatives. If you decided to take the test, here are the steps you need to follow:

Step 1: Take five sheets of paper and assign each one to an unproductive thought pattern.

Step 2: Read again every thought pattern and write for each one of them how it influenced your life in a negative way. Here is what you should know: there may be thought patterns that have influenced your life insignificantly. For these, you do not write anything, let the paper blank. But beware: you must be very sure indeed they had only a minor influence.

Step 3: Get the written papers and on the back of each sheet write the polar opposite of what you originally wrote on the paper. For example, if we consider the Unfocused Thinking pattern, where you wrote inter alia, *"I turned into an undecided person"*, you can write the polar opposite on the back *"I decided to become a determined person"*. Another example: at the Negative Thinking, if you wrote, *"I've formed a poor man thinking"*, then write on the back *"I decided to impress my mind with great emotional power, the idea of prosperity. I feel comfortable with money, as prosperity begins in my mind."*

Step 4: Transcribe all positive phrases on one sheet and simply burn all the other sheets because from that moment you started a process of change. Note that change always starts mentally and then installs in the physical plane. You will truly understand this process of change within the following laws, as I will show you step by step the process of materialization from a scientific and spiritual perspective, respectively, which allows you to re-configure your mental settings.

Step 5: What you need to do next is to wear that paper permanently with you, day after day, month after month and read it at least once a day, not in a hurry, but with a passion and a desire to change that simply defies logic. How long should you do this? I recommend that you do it at least for two months. Here is why: if you read the positive statements with a high emotional load at least once a day, you will reprogram your subconscious mind towards what you want.

What is the best time to do this? For the most effective mental programming, I recommend to you to do it at least:

- once in the morning right after you wake up and start your day, programming your mind towards what you want to become and get;

- every night before bed, because the subconscious will run during sleep these thoughts in your mind.

Through this exercise of mental reprogramming, you basically look into your life, but not in terms of what you are currently, but in terms of what you want to become. This is the right attitude because if you analyze it in terms of what you are now, then your attitude will follow the current circumstances and therefore your future results will not differ much from those of the past.

By this reprogramming exercise, your mind will minimize resistance to change, and accept change easily, since you already have planted the seeds to a new level of consciousness towards prosperity, happiness and success in the garden of your thinking. What you think today becomes tomorrow's reality.

Part 3: Summary

Before proceeding to the second law, let's repeat this law, so we leave with a very clear summary information.

The law of thought says the following: in life, in the long-term, you become exactly what you predominantly think.

The four important aspects of this law are as follows:

01. The focus of your thoughts shapes your course of action and therefore dictates your results.

02. Mental activity is not thinking.

03. You cannot stop thoughts, but you can direct them to specific objectives to produce a big difference in the results achieved in your life, and for that, you have to connect with the right people.

04. Even as of today, you can begin to act mentally, emotionally and physically in the direction of change, no matter the current conditions of your life.

Here are the most unproductive thought patterns to avoid:

- negative thinking;
- devalued thinking;
- unfocused thinking;
- small thinking;
- accusatory thinking.

LAW 2: LAW OF CONSCIOUSNESS

PART 1: SPIRITUAL DESCRIPTION OF THE LAW

Consciousness has no concrete scientific basis that can be described, unlike the first law. Trying to define consciousness is a rather complicated and inaccurate process, since there is no scientific model that can define the law. Therefore, allow me first to give you the foreground image: consciousness is the painting of your faith. Therefore, there is a strong connection between these two components, faith and consciousness. Putting your faith in thinking crystallizes your consciousness and provides spiritual power to your thinking.

I will start with a short story, which reflects quite suggestively the idea of consciousness. Here is the story:

A rich old man was being interviewed by a reporter, who asked:
"When did you start to have success?"
The old man replied to this question:
"I began to have success early when sleeping on a park bench, since at that time I already knew where I was going." [4]

This is the whole story. Basically, what did this man do? Even if he was poor, he became comfortable with the idea of success. He planted the consciousness of success in his mind, acted with great faith and thus attracted success in his life. He planted the seeds of

---
[4] Unknown author

prosperity deep in his subconscious and thus, in time, he acquired the consciousness of prosperity.

Consciousness develops as a result of the predominant mental images that govern your mind throughout life. That means you are the one who has created your own consciousness and therefore you are the one who may alter it!

When you change the predominant mental images in your mind, basically you edit your consciousness. Sure, it will not change overnight. The thoughts that you put in your mind throughout life, cannot change overnight, since the change process generally takes years.

Regarding this process of change, this is what is extremely important to understand: in life, not the change is the one that takes time, but the process of change. So, what takes time is not the change itself as the change occurs in a moment. What takes time is the process of changing and is determined by the time when you form all those abilities, making the change possible and acquiring the correct mind set towards change. We speak here of two components: skills and mental setting. This is a secret that successful people know very well, but ordinary people miss it.

The physical materialization starts with the crystallization of mental images in your own consciousness. Absolutely everything you attract in your physical life, first needs to get a clear shape in your mind. By just thinking, you are continuously producing effects. These effects appear initially as a mental thought, then, by concrete action, take physical shape. And it is absolutely correct! Think that everything man has created physically, first took a concrete shape in the mind, first crystallized in the consciousness. Thoughts are not only forms that appear in your mind and then disappear without leaving traces. When they appear in your mind, they always leave traces, but always.

If reality were different then what you let enter and run in your mind today, tomorrow you wouldn't even remember. But all those thoughts that you let run in your mind, leave traces. And all those traces form your consciousness. We will discuss the idea of consciousness in more detail, but until then we must initially discuss about the thought and the components that define it.

Thought has two components:

01. the first component is informational: is the words that you speak and if you want you can write them on paper;

02. the second is emotional: represented by the emotion attached to your thought and that you feel in your body.

For example: if you think about poverty:

- the informational component would be: "I always felt the lack of money";

- the emotional component is basically what you feel, it is the emotion attached to your thought (in this case a negative emotion of a certain intensity that you feel in your body).

As a conclusion: the thought has both an informational component and an emotional component. It is extremely important to understand this, because the only way you can change the results in your life is to initially change in your mind both components, the informational and emotional. When you change the two components, you in fact change your consciousness.

Remind yourself what I said: "change almost always starts in the non-physical plane, in the mental plane, and then installs in the physical plane." Thus, change begins in your mind, and to change your present mental representations you have only one solution: you must see, perceive, and analyze yourself, but not in terms of what you are at the moment, but in terms of what you want to become in the future, or better said, you have to perceive yourself in terms of what you want to be in your future NOW. Almost certainly, you will find this assertion very strange: in your future NOW. It is like the timeline between present and future was reduced to a single point, is like you grab the future and pull it into present. Basically, this is what you do mentally.

The statement has a lot of power, so let me help you understand it, so you can apply it correctly. To materialize your goals and not anything at chance, you have to impregnate your mind with images of what you want to have and become in the future and in the process, you have to use a lot of emotional power. Basically, you materialize the future through the power of the present. Your future starts right in the present and you crystallize in your mind the image of the future through the power of the present and this is why, the seemingly strange assertion *"in your future NOW"* really has meaning and power in the process of materialization. By this trick, you impregnate the consciousness of prosperity in your mind, when prosperity is not yet manifested in your life.

That is why it is important to apply this trick:

- if you have no money and analyze yourself in terms of what you are now, you basically impregnate your mind with the awareness of poverty more strongly;

- if you have no money, but you analyze yourself from the perspective of what you want to become, you basically impregnate your mind with the consciousness of prosperity. And so, your prosperity thoughts will become increasingly larger, while your thoughts of poverty, from lack of food, will become increasingly smaller.

This change of representation, to analyze yourself in terms of what you want to become is in fact the correct mental attitude towards a life of wealth and success. If you analyze it in terms of what you are, you actually live in the past, which then you unload it in the present and so, you materialize it in your future, by the power of the present. What you read is very strong. I recommend that you go back to this idea, because you are not reading this book for me, but you are reading it to achieve greater results, you are reading it to change your life. I am important for you only from the perspective in which I can help you, you may not even know me, but, by all of the professional techniques I have collected in this book, I can help you change your mind once and for all. I guarantee that the change in your life will occur at a high level if you apply the techniques I make available through this book.

Good! Now let us venture further with the creative thinking! I will give you two suggestive examples to gain even more understanding of this concept, called consciousness.

This is the first example:

Let's make an analogy with a computer: the platform on which you install computer programs is called Windows. The programs that you can install on your computer are determined by the performance of this platform called Windows. As it is in your case. The platform on which you install mental images of what will materialize physically is called consciousness. The results you'll get physically, are determined by the mental images in your consciousness, that your brain predominantly processes.

Here is the second example:

What is the consciousness of money?

Throughout life, your mind ran a million thoughts about money. All those thoughts have generated emotions. Well, the sum of all those thoughts and emotions determine your consciousness.

It is like painting a picture – you need to use color after color to make the whole painting, which in your case is the picture of your consciousness. Did you get the idea?

Here is the consciousness of the poor:

- to make money you must steal from others;
- to make money is very hard;
- I cannot have a lot of money;
- no one in my family had money;
- money does not bring happiness;
- must work hard for little money;
- more money means more, harder work.

Here is the consciousness of rich people:

- money is readily available;
- making money is easy;
- money is important;

- is natural to make money;
- more money means higher thinking level.

Do you understand the difference between these two kinds of people? Basically, their mental focus is located at opposite polarities. And that is why results are obtained at opposite polarities.

Let's create an overview of how consciousness develops if you sit among ordinary people: living in a world that daily fills your head with thousands of random thoughts and almost never all those thoughts help you change your mind in a manner that truly has the power to change, and you allow these thoughts to take possession of your mind. And you do it every day and so you fill up your thinking garden with negative thoughts, day after day, year after year, and they will grow increasingly larger like weeds. It is the process of planting the seeds of your own consciousness development.

You see, what you materialize physically, comes precisely from the reality that your mind knows and accepts! You may not materialize in your future a different reality until your mind sees a different reality, and for that, you have to act in this direction. Alone, it will not replace the images of what you put inside your mind as no mirror can reflect another different picture than the one which is right in front of it.

Your subconscious is like a mirror, it does not change anything that you put there, because it is not logical and never makes any assessments. The subconscious mind does not know the concept of large-small, good-bad, positive-negative. The subconscious mind does not evaluate ever. It simply fully supports what you let inside it.

Neuro Linguistic Programming and psychology are very clear in this regard.

So, if you want a different reality, you must first change your mind reality. But if you let all those random thoughts rule your mind, you will perceive reality from the perspective of a common pattern of thinking that belongs to the majority. You perceive reality within the boundaries of the only truth that your mind knows and accepts, then the reality of your mind crystallizes your consciousness that determines the attractiveness of things and events in your life. Remember that you cannot materialize in the long-term other than what falls within your consciousness. People take life as it is, they go led by the surrounding circumstances, by what happens outside them, and then they wonder why their life goes wrong.

In the process of change, you can only succeed if you get rid of those predominant thoughts that are the polar opposite of what you want and you replace them with those thoughts that lead you towards the results you desire in your life. By now, you probably are really convinced that what you attract into your life, specifically, the object of your attraction is determined by your very own consciousness.

- If you have developed the consciousness of poverty, you will attract poverty.

- If you have developed the consciousness of wealth, you will attract wealth.

- If you have developed the consciousness of disease, you will attract disease.

- If you have developed the consciousness of health, you will attract health.

So here is what the Law of Consciousness states: what you attract in your life depends on your level of consciousness regarding the object of your attraction. After years of reflection on the notion of consciousness, I managed to give it some practical representation. Be careful: when you hear, look, touch or think anything that means prosperity, success, happiness, money or anything else that comes to your emotional field of attention, are you doing it in attached or detached state?

The attached state is when you talk or hear someone else talking about prosperity, success, happiness, money, etc., and you feel that you are in harmony with those things, you feel that you belong to them, you feel good in their presence.

The detached state is the polar opposite of the attached state, specifically, you feel that there is a barrier between you and those things; you experience emotional discomfort, a state of distance.

In conclusion, if you feel the state of harmony, attachment, association, it means in fact that you are in the vibration of a certain thing, and that thing is in your vibration. This vibration causes the attraction of things and events in your life, bringing the opportunities by which these things begin to come to you. Keeping this vibration predominantly in fact, you grow the force that attracts those things in your life and thus those things will actually materialize in your life. Therefore, the source of change is right inside your mind and is determined by what you think with your emotional mind predominantly related to the object of your attraction. What governs your mind predominantly determines your consciousness.

So:

- you cannot achieve success until you first acquire consciousness of success;

- you cannot achieve prosperity until you first acquire the consciousness of prosperity;

- you cannot be in a state of perfect health, having the mind governed by the disease.

What happens basically? The way you feel predominantly in fact determines the level of your consciousness! And that's why you attract exactly what you think with the emotional mind. So, in life, you do not attract what you want, but you attract what you ARE inside you, by the thoughts you put together to form the picture of your consciousness. You are the one who has programmed the mental computer and the one who can reprogram it. You are the creator of your own reality. You create your reality with every thought you place in your mind. The thought is helping you create the reality framework and the creator of thought is in fact you.

Therefore, you cannot enjoy the wealth in the material world, unless you do not first crystallize it mentally. Mind must perceive emotionally the image of wealth in order to materialize it physically. This means that before escaping from poverty in the outside world, you first need to relieve your inner poverty buried in your subconscious that actually forms your consciousness.

Hear the words of the poor. You will find they talk about poverty, since it governs their mind and therefore their actions are oriented towards the predominant poverty. They identify mentally with poverty, emotionally live through it, poverty is part of their being, and poverty crystallizes their consciousness. Poor people build their plans to become poor, while rich people build their plans to become rich. They both build, but each at his/her level of consciousness.

What poor people do not understand is that in order to acquire wealth, they first need to replace the poverty consciousness with the prosperity consciousness in their minds. If you want to attack a problem, in fact you must attack the cause that generated it. Well, the cause of poverty is right in your mind and is determined by the poverty consciousness. Therefore, do not listen to people who get rich by various methods, but they continue to use the words of a poor man, as in the long-term they will return to poverty.

You cannot enjoy long-term wealth if you use words of a poor man, because that means you have the poverty consciousness and therefore this is what you will attract into your life; and this is very precise. Program your mental computer by poverty consciousness and that is what you will attract into your life. What you think with your emotional mind, is what materializes.

Perhaps you noticed that when I talk about consciousness, in most situations, I talk about a consciousness focused towards a particular thing, namely:

- your consciousness regarding money;
- your consciousness regarding health;
- your consciousness regarding relationships;
- your consciousness regarding success.

Basically, I did not questioned the consciousness itself, but the content of consciousness, specifically, those elements that build it. I have not discussed about the consciousness itself, as the physical manifestation should be related in fact to these components of consciousness, not to the consciousness itself.

I will give you below a mental representation of how consciousness is manifested in the physical plane: Imagine that you take a camera and make a movie with you. Then look at what you filmed. The movie is stored in the camcorder's memory and what you will see on the screen is exactly what you filmed. So it is with the results of your life. What you put into your consciousness, is exactly what will manifest in the physical plane, just as what you see on the screen is exactly the movie from the camcorder's memory.

You see, poverty is a mind disease. Physical poverty is nothing but:

- your predominant emotional expression concerning the lack of money;

- expression of your consciousness regarding the lack of money transposed in the material world;

- the image of your faith regarding poverty.

So it is with prosperity. Prosperity is an expression of your consciousness regarding money, followed by large-scale continuous action towards a well-defined objective. So what are the beliefs that you place in your consciousness? Remember what I will tell you next: your beliefs are prophecies that are going to be fulfilled. Beliefs and reality align and become one.

Faith is equivalent to the belief that you will succeed. Fear is equal to the belief that you will fail. If you've developed the belief that you will succeed, you will search for those signals that validate and confirm your belief, while ignoring all other signals which invalidate that belief. On the other hand, if you have developed the belief that you will fail, you'll search for those signals that validate this belief, while ignoring the other signals which invalidate your belief. In fact, in both cases, you're absolutely right. What differs essentially is your focus direction towards faith or fear. It is simply a choice, but in each of these cases, you're absolutely right.

Faith is in fact lack of doubt, as doubt is lack of faith. They are two concepts situated at opposite polarities. When you get close to one, you get away from the other. But please note that you cannot achieve great things with little faith. Great things can be achieved only if you have an unshakable faith, since only in this way, your mind is set to identify and capitalize on the best opportunities. Your words and mental images only have power when accompanied by faith. If you do not believe in your words, they have no power. They are like a gun without bullets.

Next, I will reveal the biggest mistake that most people make in the development of their own consciousness about what they want to materialize in their lives. They fix their mind strongly on the desire to achieve what they want: they predominantly think about what they want to achieve, talk about it day after day, and some even act following a strategy. Of course, an absolutely natural question arises:

"Where is the mistake in this process of thought and action?"

Here is the psychological process behind the action: when you think and talk about what you want from a mental standpoint, you place your object of desire somewhere in the future, outside you and plant the emotional state of desire in your thinking garden. Therefore, mentally and emotionally, you put the sign of equality between desire and what you want to achieve. And then, the Universe keeps you in this mental and emotional state, which governs your mind, specifically, it keeps you in a state of "*wanting*".

If you follow this procedure, in the best case:

- either you'll get what you want, but for a short period (you will attract it and after a while, by various life circumstances, you will lose almost everything you got);

- or you'll get only a part of the object of your desire.

But, in order to attract and maintain in the long term what you want, you need to strongly crystallize mentally and emotionally the sense of belonging, to feel that what you want is already in the process of materialization. This sense of belonging is dictated by the power of your inner faith that you will definitely get what you want.

As a conclusion, in the development of consciousness in the direction of your materialization object, you must crystallize and maintain predominantly the mental and emotional state of belonging and not the desire. The state of desire is setting the materialization object outside of your consciousness. The state of belonging is setting the materialization object inside your consciousness.

PART 2: PRACTICAL TOOL FOR LAW APPLICATION

Next, I will provide you a practical tool to help you change the level of consciousness towards what you really want. You can apply this tool every time to change your consciousness towards the direction of what you want to materialize. Changing the consciousness is a continuous process. For example, if you want to acquire the prosperity consciousness through everything you do day after day, by every experience you have, you will need to crystallize the prosperity consciousness increasingly stronger.

Visualize yourself as a rich man, feel like a rich man, see wealth around you, connect with rich people, live mentally and emotionally as a rich man and act in this way day after day, following an action plan. This is not a process to be applied for a week or a month and then you go back to the poor man's consciousness. This is a process by which you develop your prosperity consciousness increasingly stronger, at an increasingly larger scale. The process is similar for everything you want: prosperity, happiness, success, money, family, home, physical and mental health, etc.

Here are the steps of this process:

Step 1: Change your consciousness towards the direction of what you want to attract into your life.

I will detail below the process of changing your consciousness, but in reverse way, to help you understand correctly what are the steps that you must follow.

First, imagine that you are in front of a mirror and look at yourself. What you see is your image reflected in the mirror. The mirror cannot reflect another image. So it is with your mind. It cannot materialize physically other than what is in your consciousness. Therefore, you achieve in the physical plane only what corresponds to your consciousness. So, here are the steps that describe the change of consciousness:

Phase 4: To get different results, you must change your consciousness.

Phase 3: To change your consciousness, you must change the mental and emotional images in your mind.

Phase 2: To change the images, you need to change your predominant thoughts.

Phase 1: To change your thoughts, you must move to continued large-scale action that allows change.

Phase 0: In order to move to continued large-scale action, you must define clearly and specifically what you really want.

Step 2: Monitoring your level of consciousness.

This step should not be done after step 1, but at the same time as step 1, and it is a process that must be continuous. In other words, as you evolve in the process of changing consciousness, you have to assess this change. Assessment is carried out by monitoring the two states of which we spoke before in this law: detached and attached.

Here is the central idea of the consciousness monitoring process: in the process of consciousness change, you must improve the vibrational content of what you want to materialize, giving it continuous emotional attention. In this way, the level of your consciousness grows more and more until reaching a critical point, where materialization in the physical plane occurs. The idea is to continuously increase your vibrational level in order to allow you to physically materialize.

PART 3: SUMMARY

Before proceeding to the next law, let's review the essence of this law:

This is what the Law of Consciousness states:
What you attract into your life depends on your level of consciousness regarding the object of your attraction. If you're feeling attached, you're on the right track regarding the object of your attraction. If you're feeling detached, you're on the wrong track regarding the object of your attraction.

It is also important to remember: mind has two components, one informational and one emotional. Both components are important in the process of changing consciousness.

LAW 3: LAW OF ATTRACTION

PART I: SCIENTIFIC DESCRIPTION OF THE LAW

Law of Attraction states: *"You are like a magnet (because your thoughts are magnetic)"*[5] attracting exactly what you predominantly feel. From the beginning I want to create a picture for you of what you will discover in this law:

Module I – Fundamental Components of the Force of Attraction

Module II – The Right Way to Manage your Emotions

Before we venture into a detailed description of the two modules forming the Law of Attraction, I want to firstly bring the reality into the area of your knowledge. Right now, I reveal a truth to you, which at first will probably conflict with what you know. So, here is the truth: The Law of Attraction is not related to spirituality. If you've read books, listened to audio packages or watched videos, I know that most sources show the Law of Attraction as a spiritual component, but this is not true. The reason that you were left to believe so, is because this concept of attraction was not presented to you by components, but rather as a whole placed in the light of spirituality. But as you already know, the Concept of Attraction consists of two components: one scientific and one spiritual. It has real power only through the application of both components in the materialization process.

---
[5]Hicks, Esther and Jerry. *Law of Attraction. Teachings of Abraham*, Prestige Publishing House, 2007.

Presented as a whole, indeed, the best presentation perspective of this concept is really the spiritual one. But this simply is not enough. You cannot become a good runner with a missing leg. So, let's turn on the light of your consciousness and venture into a detailed description of the two modules forming the Law of Attraction.

Module I – Fundamental Components of the Force of Attraction

Three fundamental components form the force of attraction:

The first component: Thought (positive or negative)

First, I will tell you broadly what is clearly established scientifically, concerning thoughts, as Gregg Braden demonstrated in *The Divine Matrix: Bridging Time, Space, Miracles, and Belief*:

- Any thought can be measured and displayed on a computer as electromagnetic signal, similar to that emitted by your cell phone.

- Every thought is transmitted almost instantaneously over large distances, distances that exceed the size of the Earth.

- Thought is a form of energy that works inside and outside your mind, creating resonance processes with the other so-called similar thoughts.

Said in a simple form: your thought resonates, interferes with similar thoughts generated by other people. It's like throwing two stones into a lake at the same time. The waves formed interfere. So it is with people's thoughts, those alike interfere.

Therefore, you emit a strong and persistent thought in the Universe, where your thought is in magnetic resonance with other similar thoughts. Resonance refers to the interference of your thought with similar thoughts, of the same nature. This is why you attract certain people in your life. The scientific explanation is shown exactly by those mental resonance phenomena between your thoughts and the thoughts of others. You've probably heard this expression before: Birds of a feather flock together. So it is, but why do they come together: for they think about the same, they emit similar vibrations that generate resonance phenomena.

Let's summarize what we know so far in a simple form:

- thought is an electromagnetic signal that can be measured;
- thought is transmitted over long distances;
- every thought interferes with other similar thoughts.

So far, we have discussed the first component of the force of attraction – thought, which can be positive or negative.

The second component: Emotional State

Emotional state is the physiological reaction of your thought. The thought that you emit, you perceive it physiologically into your body as an emotional state. Well, the emotional state lets you know how well you are focused in relation to what you want. A positive emotional state lets you know that you are well focused in relation to what you want. A negative emotional state lets you know that you are in bad focus compared to what you want. So, how you feel indicates your positioning in relation to what you want.

You cannot directly monitor the thoughts you have. But there is a shortcut that lets you know if your thought is positive or negative. And this shortcut is actually your emotional state. When the connection between thought and emotion is very strong, it turns into belief. So, the belief is an energy invisible to the human eye, which indicates the strength of your faith. To produce changes in the physical plane, you must first change this invisible energy. Your beliefs are the ones that can change this energy. Emotions are the tool that shows you how well you are focused in relation to what you want, indicate your relationship with your inner being, and indicate how well you are aligned between what you say you want and your inner emotional state.[6]

The time of materialization of what you want is mainly determined by the alignment between what you think and what you feel. Alignment is a combination of two states: a state of emotional release combined with a state of great faith. These two states must live in you when you have thoughts directed towards what you want. If these two states are living in you, then you are aligned!

In conclusion, so far we have discussed the first two components of the force of attraction:

First component: the thought that you emit, positive or negative;

---

[6]See: Byrne, Rhonda. *The Secret*. Adevar Divin Publishing House, Braşov, 2007, p.62

Second component: the emotional state attached to your thought, which lets you know how well you are positioned in relation to what you want.

The third component: Materialization

Materialization is in fact a result of the resonance processes. The process is purely scientific. What you feel predominantly will materialize in your life. From the start, here is the secret of this step: you must keep active your emotional state corresponding to what you want, until it materializes.

If in the first two steps, "*Thought*" and "*Emotional state*", you generated the force of attraction, well, in the last step "*Materialization*", you basically keep active this force so as to attract what you want. Therefore, what you need to do is to continuously add emotional load towards what you want. Otherwise, you will interrupt the process of materialization, because you generated the force of attraction and practically you attached what you want at vibrational level, but you have not maintained this force, which materializes the object of your desire in the physical plane. Here is an example: if you throw the ball into a wall, it returns to you. However, the ball will return to you unless you left from where you threw it.

How long does the process of materialization takes?
Since this is one of the most common questions asked by the majority, let's give it due consideration and start with a suggestive story:

A man who wanted to reach the next village, was walking through the forest when he realized he was lost. And after wandering through the woods, he saw a woodcutter, approached him and happily he asked:

"Tell me sir, in what direction is the next village?"

And the woodcutter showed him the direction by pointing with his arm.

Gladly, the man thanked him and then asked:

"But how many hours do I have to walk to reach the village?"

The woodcutter looked at him and said nothing. Then he continued to cut wood.

And then the man asked again:

"Sir, tell me how many hours do I have to walk to reach the village?" The woodcutter looked at him and said nothing. Then he continued to cut wood.

Surprised by the reaction of the woodcutter, the man said in his mind:

"He acts as if he were deaf, so I ask him for the last time:

"Sir, tell me how many hours do I have to walk to reach the village?"

The woodcutter looked at him and said nothing. Then he continued to cut wood.

The man leaves wondering about the woodcutter's reaction and after about 30 meters, the woodcutter replies: two hours. And then, the man returned surprised to the woodcutter and asked:

"But why didn't you tell me when I was close to you?"

And the woodcutter answered:

"Because I had to see how fast you walk!"[7]

The situation in the process of materialization is similar: it depends on how much emotional load you put in this process and how often, and it depends on how well aligned you are with respect to what you want to

---
[7] unknown author

materialize. If you let doubt creep into your mind, it will take you longer, and if doubt dominates your mind, then you will fail to materialize what you want. In other words, the speed of materialization depends on you; you are the source of materialization, by the power of your emotional thought firmly focused!

If you remember, I said from the beginning that the secret of this step, called materialization, is to keep active the emotional state and therefore the force of attraction. Now, let's strengthen this representation. Specifically: how do you actively maintain this force? Keeping the force of attraction active means to focus on the ultimate goal. Focusing on the ultimate goal is an extremely important aspect of this law without which the force of attraction will be very small.

So:
"What does it mean to focus on the ultimate goal?"
This process consists of generating the emotional state that you would have after you've already got what you want. Stay focused predominantly on this state, lock it emotionally inside your body. This state should be similar to that of a child when expecting the present under the Christmas tree. The child is continuously waiting as certainly knows that he/she will receive the present under the Christmas tree. He/she does not know exactly when, but he/she is confident this will happen and that is why he/she is in a state of continuous focus on the ultimate goal.

In order to have an accurate picture, I'll give you some examples. The focus on the ultimate goal refers to the following:

- focus on what you will do with the money after you get it;

- focus on the emotional state that you will have after you get the car that you desire;

- focus on how you will live after you get your perfect health;

- focus on your attitude after you get the job you want.

Basically, focusing on the ultimate goal, is to feel that you've already got what you want. So, you have to generate the emotional state by which you feel that what you want is already yours. It is extremely important to understand this aspect of the law and reprogram your thinking in this way.

I will give you below a very specific example of focusing on the ultimate goal, focus towards money. Here is how it works:

If you say every day: "I want to have money!"
Perhaps you think this is a positive thought! But it is not! If you repeat daily: "*I want to have more money*", then your mind actually recognizes and accepts that what you want, is missing from your life. You basically generate thoughts of laking. Thus, you give more power to the lack of money and basically send the money away from yourself. You actually honor the truth that your mind knows that you live a life that is full of lacking. If you want money, don't set the goal on "*I want to ...*" as the Universe will maintain the mental state of "*wanting*". And as you repeat every day "*I want to ...*", the Universe will bring into manifestation through resonance phenomena exactly what you asked for and so will leave you "*to want*" and "*to want*" and "*to want*" forever, because this is what you in fact asked for. If you want money, then set your target in a very specific form:

"I am so grateful NOW because I collected EUR 200,000. I thank the divine creating power for this money. Money and I live in total harmony."

Do you understand the difference? In this situation, you project yourself mentally and emotionally in the state in which you already have money and your subconscious does not know the difference between imagination and reality, and it will provide the best solutions to bring you the money that you asked for. The subconscious mind does not think. It only accepts the images you project on the mental screen.

If you set the wrong target (for example: "I want to have more money"), your subconscious mind may not assign any image of your desire, because it does not know what "*a lot of money*" means to you. With the subconscious mind you must work very specifically, to provide clear information, to tell it exactly how much money you want and why you need that money, but not evasive answers like: I want money to live better and to have something to spend.

In conclusion, the three fundamental elements of the force of attraction are thought, emotional state and materialization.

Module II – The Right Way to Manage your Emotions

The process itself described in the first module is quite simple, and anyone applies it. Basically, you generate a thought and feel an emotional state that, if you keep it active, you will create the conditions of the physical materialization of what you want. Sure, you could say this is after all an absolutely natural process, which until now you performed anyway. You may not realize the steps of this process, but you were doing it anyway. So, here, is no challenge!

The real challenge is managing emotions. I do not want to accuse anyone of lack of emotional control, nor present a truncated reality. So here is the truth: most people are in a state of numbed mental and emotional awakening. In any book of emotional intelligence you read, regardless of the author, you will discover this truth. For some, the reality is even more painful: they are in a state of emotional retardation! Any challenge that arises in their lives throws them down mentally and emotionally. I am sorry to say this, but it is simply the truth. And I prefer to tell you the truth, as the process of change starts from awareness. You cannot solve a problem unless you first realize it. I do not want to deceive you using beautiful words, so let me introduce you to the reality. Most people need more help, more education regarding the acquisition of emotional control and the impact of the emotional control over the outcomes of their lives.

The level at which you are in terms of emotional control is dictated by how you react under stress and pressure, and when you make important decisions in life. Your level of emotional control is not determined by how you react under normal conditions, when all is well and good around you. I say this because most people think they have very good emotional control, when in fact they evaluate themselves in everyday situations in which everything is fine and pretty. What these people do is not called self-assessment, but overvaluation. But overvaluation does not provide an accurate picture of their emotional level, and under pressure they react disastrously and reach disappointments and sometimes even depression.

Experts argue that emotional intelligence is responsible for about 60-70% of success. Do you think it's a coincidence that successful people have reached very good emotional control? Of course that is not a coincidence! This is actually a practical confirmation of the fact that 60-70% of success in life is dictated by emotional control. Put in a very simple form: your prevalent emotions determine your success or failure.

Good! Let's continue: who determines your emotions?
Here is the answer: the thoughts you have.
So, thoughts determine your emotions. Emotions are actually the physiological response to the thoughts you have. And that is why you become exactly what you predominantly think with your emotional mind.

Regarding the negative thoughts, there are two major sources of negative influence:

- the first source is the influence of your own thoughts;
- the second source is the influence of outsiders on you.

Both are harmful to you. Therefore, to achieve positive thinking it is not enough just to put your own thoughts in order, but you must become selective with the people you choose to spend most of your time.

Here is a powerful truth: when you put your thoughts in order, then you put your emotions in order and then your emotional control will increase continuously. So it is no accident that emotions are basically the foundation of the Law of Attraction.

Here is the interesting part related to emotions: emotional control does not depend on what happens in your life, whereas approximately 10% is related to the event itself, and 90% is related to how you react to that event in accordance with the author and motivational speaker,

Stephen Covey. We speak here of two components: the event itself and how you react to the event. But how you react depends on your mental processes, your mindset, in other words it depends on you! You can make that unpleasant event the center of your life and generate negative emotions, or you can choose to watch the event from a perspective that keeps you in a state of emotional power.

You know what? You may not always change what is happening outside you (the event itself and the people around you), but you can always, but always, change what happens to you (how you react to the event). So, do not try to control what is not up to you, (the exterior, circumstances in your life), but only control what is up to you, (the interior). And then, you discover that the exterior begins to align with your interior.

If you identify yourself by the present circumstances in your life, you basically program yourself mentally to benefit from the same set of circumstances in your future, because what you set in your mind is the image of these circumstances. If you let yourself be led predominantly by the circumstances of your life, then what is happening outside of you becomes stronger than what happens in you. Be extremely careful with what follows, because it is very powerful for your life. What your mind interprets as external reality is in fact your interior mirror. The way you choose to see the outside world, creates the reality your mind knows and accepts, and you will manifest precisely this reality in the physical plane.

Let's create more clarity on the mental screen.
To make myself better understood, as to the correct management of emotions, I'll start with a question:

"How do you know that a thought is positive or negative?"

Basically, there is a reference for comparison: good or bad. In addition, there is no defined boundary between good and evil. That makes you think, doesn't it?

This is the thought monitoring process: the emotional state is the one that lets you know how well you are positioned in relation to what you want. So what you should monitor in the state of materialization is actually the emotional status attached to your thought and not the thought itself. Emotional state is the only gate you have, so that you become aware of your position in relation to what you want.

Think hard about what follows: let's think that people would be deprived of this indicator called emotion. What do you think would happen? How would it be to live in a world where emotion disappears? Can you imagine such a world? If emotional state disappears, you will basically have absolutely no reference system by which to define whether you have a positive or negative thought. In conclusion, what you need to monitor in fact is the emotional state.

Let's talk further about a big trap in managing emotions! Be very careful not to fall into it. I myself have tested it consciously, to check how the mind and body respond. So I do not recommend that you even test it. There are people who from a desire to focus on positive emotions have a natural tendency to slip into a big trap: they try to block their negative emotional states, virtually destroying their emotional guidance system. The goal is not to become insensitive to what is negative, because in fact, you must become sensitive to emotions.

The goal is to identify your emotion and:

- if positive, then amplify your mood, feel stronger;
- if negative, reduce its size, don't pay attention, redirect your thoughts immediately to what you really want.

Therefore, you have to think constantly about what you do and do not want. How would you expect to achieve results, thinking exactly about what you do not want, that is the polar opposite of what drives you towards results?

Remember what we discussed regarding the Law of Thinking: rich people think of wealth, poor people think of poverty, sick people think of disease, faithful people think of faith, and successful people think of success. They talk about it, put emotional load in this and therefore they obtain it. Basically, they focus their emotional attention towards what they want and in no case in the direction of what they do not want! So change your thinking from what you don't want and place all your emotional load to what you really want.

You see, the Law of Attraction does not consider whether you generate a positive or negative thought. The Law only brings into manifestation what corresponds to your predominant emotional state. What you feel predominantly will materialize on the physical plane.

How do you attract a chain of negative events?

Surely you had days or periods in life when negative things were coming at you one after another. The process was like a chain reaction. Here is how it works: a chain reaction always starts with a negative thought, to which you give increasingly more attention, more emotional nourishment. This psychological process automatically positions you in a negative emotional state corresponding to your thought.

Furthermore, this emotional state will trigger in your mind similar emotions from other similar thoughts. It's like an experience leads to the next and then a negative thought is joined by other negative thoughts.

The more negative thoughts you gather, the more you position yourself in an emotional state that is amplified. Basically, that first negative thought you run in your mind, to which you give increasingly more emotional attention, is the trigger for the chain reaction that positions you on a frequency specific to negative situations. Then, as you react to that situation, you create conditions to attract more similar situations and that is why I mentioned above that an experience leads to the next .

Question: "How much time does this reaction remains active?"
Answer: "Until you change the focus of your thoughts and emotion in the direction of what you want."

Until then you're running around like in a carousel and you wonder why more negative things are manifesting increasingly in your life. And, as you ask yourself this question, you throw the blame on bad luck or lack of luck. But you create your own luck, it is in fact the intersection of skills and opportunity as Lucius Seneca said: *"Luck is what happens when preparation meets opportunity."* When the two conditions are simultaneously achieved, results appear, which some label as an emblem called luck. The roman emperor Marcus Aurelius said,

"The happiness of your life depends upon the quality of your thoughts." Now you already know the process by which you attract chain events. So you're qualified to pass to the next stage.

How do you keep your Negative Thoughts away from your mind?

Perhaps you expect a process with high difficulty that only a small proportion of people can understand and apply. But you will not believe how simple it is as a process itself. So how do you keep negative thoughts away?

Here is the answer: if you want to stop negative thoughts, just plant only positive thoughts in your mind. Do not try to resist negative thoughts, because in this way you actually activate the vibration of what you do not want. Do not oppose them, but let them go just like clouds in the sky. Just plant positive thoughts in the garden of your thinking. When negative thoughts arise, do not pay attention, change your course immediately and focus on what you really want. As you repeat this process, you'll reduce increasingly your negative thoughts that will die because of lack of emotional nourishment, while positive thoughts will become increasingly larger. So, while negative thinking is silenced, positive thinking is increased and thus you will attract increasingly more of what you want.

What is a negative emotion?

As an example, we will discuss a concrete situation: let's consider going to a meeting where you hear someone talking about money. While you listen, you feel a negative emotion, which physiologically you perceive through emotional discomfort. This negative state lets you know that in your subconscious mind there is a number of programs called mental beliefs that oppose your desire to have money. This means that in your mind, you have not crystallized the consciousness of money, you still do not live mentally and emotionally in harmony with the idea of money. Basically, negative emotional state informs you that in your mind there are powerful programs that stop the attraction of money in your life. When you see, hear, experience, anything that your subconscious mind is not in harmony with, you feel a negative emotional state. On the other hand, when you see, hear, experience, anything that your subconscious mind is in harmony with, you feel a positive emotional state. Basically, a positive or negative emotional state lets you know whether you are or not in harmony with a certain thing.

When a negative thought appears in your mind, you feel a negative emotion. I recommend that you change such a thought immediately. Imagine that negative thought burning like a piece of paper and immediately replace it with a positive thought. This is why I recommend that you do this immediately: because at the beginning, thought and emotion are of low intensity and easy to replace. If you pay attention, they become bigger and they will be much harder to replace. You will need more powerful techniques, it will take more time and it will consume more positive energy in order to cancel the negative energy. But if you apply the replacement strategy immediately even if you have no experience in these psychological processes, you'll very easily replace that negative thought, as it has no power. It gets power only if you provide emotional nourishment.

You should again pay attention to this strategy. Its impact is fabulous over years, because it starves your negative thinking so hard that it no longer has real power in your life. Even if your past was painful through the events you attracted, I have good news for you: No matter what level you are at the moment, your future starts today and thus you can make a big change in your life, you can shape the future by what you think and do, starting today. The mere fact that you have purchased this book is not a coincidence. Inside your mind, there is a strong desire for change.

Every thought you have, generates an emotional state that can range from unnoticeable to very strong. Think about when you passed an exam: you generated a thought and felt an emotional state. So it is when you think about a public discussion or to pay bills, etc.
Think of poverty! What do you feel?
Think about when you were in love? What do you feel?
Do you get the idea?

So you cannot deliver a thought without that thought being accompanied by an emotional state. Emotion attached to your thought determines the physical materialization, and the results you get. Thought and emotion work together, you cannot separate them. What you can do is just change the emotional load attached to your thought.

Here is the process by which you attract negative events in your life:

Step 1: you focus your thoughts in the direction of what you do not want;

Step 2: these thoughts generate negative emotional states in you;

Step 3: negative emotional states create conditions by resonance phenomena through which you attract more of what you do not want;

Step 4: when you attract more of what you do not want, negative emotional states will grow and you will actually go back to step 1, except that, this time, your thoughts and emotions will get into an amplified negative state.

If you have fallen into this trap, you actually follow what I call *"the hamster's tour"* and the only way to get out of this trap is not to fight the negative, but focus on positive things.

Here is the process by which you attract positive events to your life:

Step 1: focus your thoughts towards positive things;

Step 2: these thoughts generate positive emotions;

Step 3: positive emotional states create conditions by resonance phenomena, through which you attract more positive events;

Step 4: when you attract more positive events, the emotional states attached will grow so you will actually go back to *step 1*, only this time your thoughts and emotions will get into an amplified positive state.

In conclusion: you find yourself constantly under the influence of emotions, which actually determine the manifestation of all the cells in your body.[8]

---

[8] Arntz, William., Chasse, Betsy., Vicente, Mark. *What the Bleep Do We Know?!*, Carte Daath Publishing House, Bucharest, 2007

This is why people who have developed positive thinking are in good health and attract positive results. People who have developed negative thinking are generally sick and attract all kinds of unfortunate events in their lives.

Here is how that happens: your emotional state dictates the strength of your immune system through substances called neuropeptides, which are neurotransmitters between the brain and the rest of your body. When your mind is flooded with sadness, stress, anxiety, depression, those neuropeptides send signals to your body to reduce the energy that is used to fight off disease. The energy drop weakens your immune system, which makes you vulnerable to disease, from a simple cold to serious forms of cancer.

If your mind currently runs the same mental programs as in the past, basically, you will relive the same emotions and if you do not change emotions in your body, the cell degrades. Yesterday's thoughts pollute your future, so I recommend that you disconnect from the old mental programs.

Convincing scientific evidence on the link between mind and body come from dr. Candace Pert, who studied the effects of mind and emotions on health.

Her research focused on the biochemical substances called neuropeptides, which were discovered to be messenger molecules that carry signals from the brain to every cell in the body. Dr. Candace Pert discovered that neuropeptides act as keys that fit locks, specific areas on cells called receptors. Receptors have been shown to cover the surface of all cells in the body, including the immune system. According to the research of Dr. Candace Pert, neuropeptides transmit orders for our emotions. Thus, if a person is happy, sad or furious, some neuropeptides transmit that feeling throughout the body.

To go further, here is the question:
"Who influences your emotional state?"
Here is the answer: you influence your emotional state by thoughts which predominantly govern your mind.

Your emotional state has power over your DNA. Human DNA has an impressive amount of information, but most of that information is inactive. Your emotional states can enable or disable an impressive number of genes. Positive emotions activate a large number of genes while negative emotions disable a large number of genes, and close sequences at the genetic level. If positive emotions relax the DNA, negative emotions will shrink it, as demonstrated by Gregg Braden, The Divine Matrix: Bridging Time, Space, Miracles, and Belief. For example: laughter generates a positive emotional state that can activate up to 23 genes that are normally inactive. DNA responds with amazing accuracy to the emotions that you generate.

When you feel an emotion that fills your body and a passion that defies logic, you actually release a great power of attraction. This is the worst part: most people invest their emotions in and speak passionately about the negative. They focus a great power of attraction towards things that they do not want in their lives. Rather than create the reality they want, they create the reality they don't. Rather than live their dream they live their nightmare.

PART 2: PRACTICAL TOOLS FOR LAW APPLICATION

Under this law, I will be extremely generous to you and I will give you three practical tools to apply:

- the first two tools are intended to monitor your subconscious thoughts;

- the third tool aims at changing the predominant thoughts that govern your mind.

The purpose of these tools is to monitor and change the direction of focus of your predominant thoughts that produce the greatest results in your life.

Tool for monitoring your subconscious thoughts – version 1

This instrument consists of a process that takes place in 4 steps:

Step 1: Darken the room and place a candle (preferably a taller one, 10-20 cm) on a table.

Step 2: Put some music on that gently brings you into a state of deep relaxation.

Step 3: Sit in a comfortable position at about 1.5-2 meters away from the candle. Your eyes should be at the same level with the candle so as to look straight ahead.

Step 4: Set yourself a time of 20 minutes in which to carry out the following mental process:

a) look constantly at the candle flame trying to empty your mind, not think about anything, enter a deep state of relaxation. The great secret is to try as much as possible not to think about anything.

b) try to blink increasingly rarely, while your gaze seeks the candle flame.

The psychological process of this 4-step tool consists of minimizing the activity of your conscious mind and be brought into a state of deep relaxation. Basically, try to remove your conscious thought from your framework as much as possible and thus, your mind will primarily access subconscious thoughts brought into your conscious mind.

How many days do you have to do this exercise?
For the right result I recommend that you do this every day for a week. You will become aware of the predominant thoughts that govern your mind, and what governs your mind, you will attract in the physical plane. What you actually materialize is the reflection of your conscious image.

Tool for monitoring your subconscious thoughts – version 2

This tool consists of a process that takes place in two steps:

Step 1: Pay attention to your thoughts in the first 5 minutes when you wake up every morning.

What you think in the first 5 minutes are the most powerful thoughts which will set your direction in life for the coming years, if you continue with the same mindset and activities, as they determine the direction of movement through life. They might be called first-class thoughts, dominant, the most powerful, those which set your direction of travel.

Step 2: Pay attention to your predominant thoughts during the day while you perform common tasks.

Your thoughts during the day are in fact thoughts to which you pay attention normally and they dictate the size of results corresponding to your direction. These thoughts are attached to your predominant actions. These thoughts could be called second-class thoughts, essential.

To be sure that my message reaches you correctly, I create now a visual representation of the two categories of thoughts for you. Consider that you go by car from location A to location B and on this route you must pass through 5 cities. Between the two locations you will see several signs. The signs that give you information about the direction of travel from one city to the next, we consider primary signs corresponding to the first category of thoughts, the dominant ones. They act as milestones and determine your direction of travel.

On the other hand, we consider the signs that warn you of possible restrictions, road hazards and other obligations, secondary signs corresponding to the second category of thoughts, the essential ones. They correspond to activities that you have to do between the milestones and determine the size of results in your life.

In conclusion:

- Primary signs set your direction of travel from one city to the next; they correspond to the physical direction in which you are going in life in the coming years if you continue to think the same thoughts as before;

- Secondary signs warn you of possible restrictions, road hazards and other obligations; they correspond to physical actions between the milestones that determine the size of your results.

How many days do you have to do this exercise?
Do it frequently as it does not involve the allocation of special time. You monitor your thoughts while doing normal activities and the process itself is extremely simple. All you have to do is just become more aware of the thoughts you have. After a few months of the aware application of this monitoring process, you'll reach the stage where you do it reflexively.

Tools for changing the predominant thoughts

This tool aims at changing the predominant thoughts that govern your mind and actually make your consciousness. This tool requires the investment of time on your part. You may say that you do not have time, I understand and that is why let me ask you a question from my soul:
"How long from today will you decide that you do not have time?"
You can hide behind this reason, which is currently perhaps the painful reality of your life materialized by the power of your thinking. You can do this, but in a few years, you'll say again that you have no time.
And then, you will return mentally to the question I asked above:
"How long from today will you decide that you do not have time?"

You get the idea? I hope that you are careful enough to say "YES".
So, let's get to action because the change I propose is at a higher level and aims at changing the direction of focus of your predominant thoughts.

Here is the action plan:

Step 1: Determine the most important areas of your life. To help you, I will tell you which are the most important areas for most people, and you will establish whether they are applicable in your case. Analyze and modify where necessary.

Here are the most important areas: career, money, health, spirituality, family, personal development.

Step 2: Write each important area on a piece of flip-chart paper (it is important to be a large sheet) and then determine three types of objectives for each area of action, specifically in the following order:

- Long-term goals (10 years);
- Mid-term goals (5 years);
- Short-term goals (1-2 years).

Important: short-term goals should reflect the mid-term goals and mid-term goals should support the long-term goals. Thus, you get a tree of goals. Do not think you will realize this structure in a few hours. You may need even weeks. The advantage of this structure is that it will direct your predominant thoughts and physical, emotional and intellectual energy to what is truly important in your life. Otherwise, you go through life randomly, with no clear direction.

Step 3: Buy yourself a book of dreams, then consider every object in your action plan as a dream. Write it in the book of dreams and set a deadline. The Book of Dreams is a book of unwritten sheets since you are the creator of your future, so you will need to complete it with your dreams and goals.

Step 4: Every day, think predominantly about your dreams, put as much emotional load in this process, as it will direct your energy toward what you want. You will starve your thoughts and emotions related to what you do not want.

Step 5: This step refers to action and we will detail it in the last law, of the Organized Plan. First, you need to understand the strategies governing the Law of the Organized Plan and then move on to concrete action towards your goals.

PART 3: SUMMARY

Now in the end, let's repeat the most important aspects of this law:

- Here is what the Law of Attraction states: You are like a magnet (because your thoughts are of magnetic nature) that attracts exactly what you predominantly feel.

- The three fundamental elements of the force of attraction are thought, emotional state and materialization.

- Regarding the right way to manage your emotions: how do you keep negative thoughts out of your mind? Simply: plant positive thoughts in your thinking garden and do not pay attention to your negative thoughts, change your direction of focus immediately from what you do not want and place all emotional load on what you really want.

LAW 4: LAW OF LEAST RESISTANCE

PART I: SCIENTIFIC DESCRIPTION OF THE LAW

"Much unhappiness in your life is because you obey your inner self instead of communicating with it."[9]

"What is the meaning of this phrase full of wisdom?"
Most people, when having negative thoughts, let those thoughts to run in their minds on autopilot, again and again, day after day. Thus, those negative thoughts become increasingly larger, as they are fed emotionally. If we look deeper at Martyn Lloyd Jones's statement, we find that he speaks of two mental processes:

01. Listening: "Obey your inner self";
02. Communication: "Instead of communicating with it."

So, most people accept the thoughts that enter their minds but they do not communicate with them. Communication with those random thoughts tends to be zero. Simply, they leave those thoughts to enter and run in their minds. Instead of communicating with those thoughts, wondering where they come from, what direction they lead to, what is the benefit of running those thoughts, they simply accept them exactly as they are and thus, those thoughts become the very reality their mind knows and accepts. These are people who react to life instead of acting!

---
[9] Jones, Martyn Lloyd – *Spiritual depression,* Perla Suferintei Publishing House, Suceava, 2006

I tell you without reservation: two mental attitudes of opposite polarities "*to act*" and "*to react*" govern your whole life, whether you want it or not, whether you like it or not. So what is the difference between "*acting*" and "*reacting*" and in which direction does each of them drive you?

For a proper understanding, let's make a comparison between the two mental attitudes:

- to act involves: being in control of your emotions;
- to react involves: to let emotions control you.

- to act: what happens in you is more powerful than what is happening outside of you;
- to react: what happens outside you controls what happens inside you.

- acting involves: thinking;
- reacting involves: accessing a database in the brain called the memory.

- acting involves: perceiving reality through a positive attitude that leads to growth;
- reacting involves: perceiving reality through a negative attitude that leads to collapse.

So, those who react see a real problem in every event which becomes their emotional focus. On the other hand, those who act, see a challenge in every event, a new teacher of life.

Allow me to create for you greater clarity by the following practical example:
"Is the world good or bad?"
Think about it from your perspective, not from what others say:
"Is the world good or bad?"

For some, the world is a real machine of mental, physical and emotional torture. For others, the world is like the sky filled with stars. Yet the reality? They both live in the same world. However, what makes the difference? Well, the difference is your perception of the world and world relation with you. But relation of the world with you is largely determined by your perception of the world, which is determined by the attitude you have regarding the world.

Barry Neil Kaufman said: "*The way we choose to see the world, creates the world as we see it.*" When the mind heals, the outside world heals too. Those who react, see the world as evil, as a machine of torture. Those who act, see the world as good.

Those who react, believe that what is happening in the outside world determines their results in life. Thus, they are in a constant struggle with the outside world and bring negative emotional load into this process. On the other hand, those who act, believe their results are dictated by their own way of thinking and acting. And therefore, they are powerful, because they control the emotions, decisions and actions they make.

So:

- those who react, see life as a bitterness and for this reason they fight with everything going on around them, they resist;

- those who act are in control, they eliminated the resistance, their life is a smooth flow of events, like a river.

As we venture further into the understanding of this law, let's summarize what we have discussed so far:

- "*To react*" involves letting your thoughts run in your mind randomly, that means you place your thinking in autopilot;

- "*To act*" involves thinking, to wake your own consciousness, to get control of your emotions, decisions and actions and therefore control of your life results.

So far, we have brought two mental settings into the light of knowledge, through a comparative analysis: to act or react. Here is what you have to know because it is very important: there are two ways to react:

Method 1: Fight

If you fight with the events in your life, you meet a lot of obstacles, a lot of problems will manifest in your life and you will be filled with problems. So you will only attract more trouble.

The reality is that the average man enters battle with life, day after day. First he/she complicates life hard enough, then, while trying to find solutions he/she gets involved in what complicated it, until reaching a paralyzed state of thought and action. Once in this desperate state and devoid of solutions, he/she begins to blame other people, the destiny, God, the circumstances of his/her life.

The primary mental activity of the common man is to identify enough reasons to grieve, to fight with life, react as he was so "*educated*" by parents, classical educational system, current social environment, sources of mass manipulation. However, it is not a process of creative education in which man used his own judgment, but rather a process of mechanization of thought, through which it has been circulated often enough, the idea that life must be a constant struggle with all that surrounds him.

If the common man believes that life is a struggle, then the absolutely natural question arises: Who is the opponent? He has virtually no opponent and against whom is he fighting, against whom exerts so much life resistance? The answer is one: against himself. The ordinary man generates for himself large mental and emotional damage; for him life is a continuous war.

If your mind operates in this position, of the fight, you'll be creating conditions to attract more people, events and circumstances allowing struggle to make room in your life. And as they make their way, your beliefs about the fact that life is a struggle, become increasingly powerful, and you will perceive reality through this mechanism, of the fight and you can always justify this way of thinking and action.

To escape from this trap, you have to bring peace into your mind and heart, you must pass from the phase of "*to react*" into the phase "*to act*". How do you do that? When a less pleasant event occurs in your life, you should not fight it as to fight leads to mental, emotional and physical wear. See the event as a challenge through which you can move to a higher level of mental and emotional development, to a new level of knowledge and wisdom. The challenges are made to be overcome and any challenge is a new life teacher.

Method 2: Flight

By flight, you try to avoid a situation, an unpleasant event, in which case such situation will follow you just like a shadow, and in fact you will meet again and again with the situation or similar situations, since the problem is in your mind, and you cannot run away leaving behind your mental programs. By running you have not eliminated the problem, but you just tried to avoid it by running.

In conclusion:

- if you try to fight the events of your life, you will attract more fighting;

- if you try to run, those events will follow you like a shadow and you will meet them again in the future.

When you try to resist life, to fight, to fight back, you basically break the law of least resistance. What your mind sees is the fight and therefore you will attract fighting into your life as the mind materializes physically exactly what falls within the boundaries of its thought.

The goal is not to resist as much to what you do not like, because in this mode you activate the vibration of what you do not want. The purpose is to oppose minimum resistance. When problems arise in life, if you react by fight or flight, you'll encounter more problems in the future. And then, you'll react to the new problems, you'll feed them with negative thoughts, and they will become increasingly larger.

PART 2: PRACTICAL TOOL FOR LAW APPLICATION

Tool 1: Change your thoughts and emotional energy

Furthermore, I offer you a way to change the thoughts and emotional energy, which consists of focusing your attention on positive things. How do you do that? No matter where you are, who you interact with, what do you do, you must have a clear intention in your mind: to program your mind to simply look for positive things, while you ignore the negative and do not give them conscious attention.

It is possible that the person you are talking to, has a lot of things that bother you, but certainly there are some positive things to like about that person, so ask yourself:
"What positive qualities do I like in this person?"
Find immediate answers and focus your discussion on relying on those positive qualities.

This mental process keeps your mind focused on positive things and automatically your behavior towards that person will change, the way you talk will change, the whole relationship with that person will change. I guarantee that this technique will make an amazing difference in how well you get along with others. You and the person you talk to, will feel positive and therefore will both gain, since you minimized the resistance to what you do not like.

Tool 2: Action Awareness

Let me help you from a practical perspective: Next, I will provide you a tool extremely easy to apply, but with great power of transforming your life. It contains a set of four questions that will help you realize immediately if your actions produce tangible results, or if you are just wasting your time and energy on random activities. I assure you: the more often you use this tool the more control of your life you will get.

Here are the four questions:

Question 1: What am I doing now?
The purpose of the question: helps you clarify your mind about everyday actions, to become aware and accountable for your decisions.

Question 2: Why am I doing this?
The purpose of the question: helps you clearly identify the reasons for doing that action, so you'll be able to avoid activities that do not bring you results. Your mind will enter into a state of awareness, you will not engage in actions at random.

Question 3: Where am I going?
The purpose of the question: helps you define very specific benefits (of any kind) that you have from your action. To take an action without seeking concrete results is to take an action without direction. In life, if you act without direction, you'll get nowhere. It is like a plane taking off, and at 10 km of altitude, the pilot announces that he will set a destination at random after he'll decide.

Question 4: What will happen when I get there?
The purpose of the question: keeps you focused on the things that are really important to you in the long term.

Next, let's discuss a specific example, in a life-related context. Suppose you are in a car going to a meeting.

Question 1: What am I doing now?
I am going to meet with person X and is my decision because I have a very clear purpose.

Question 2: Why am I doing this?
Because I am interested in strengthening the relationship with person X, to build a project together.

Question 3: Where am I going?
First I want to build trust and then to set the details of our project.

Question 4: What will happen when I get there?
The project is the first step in opening a new business in which we engage together because only together we can achieve results that bring us contentment.

Well, this 4-step process can be applied in any context in your life. If you make it a habit, you'll be surprised to discover what enormous difference it will produce in the long-term, in terms of mental clarity, the decisions you take and hence the results. In addition, it does not cost anything to do this, but it will cost you a lot if you do activities without a direction.

I am sure you won't follow this 4-step process in 100% of your actions. Nobody does that in 100% of the actions, I do not do it 100%, you will not do it 100%. However, it is sufficient to apply this technique to the most important actions and this will produce a big difference. This simple strategy will keep you in a positive state, full of energy, which will direct your thinking to what you want and you will attract more of what you want. This strategy produces a radical change in your dominant vibration this will minimize the resistance with which you oppose life.

As you may have realized, the results of your life are mainly determined by strategy and continuity. Those who reach great results in life do not have a potential different from yours, but a different strategy and regularly follow it day after day. They succeed, but not because they have a potential far above average, they succeed because their perseverance is well above average.

PART 3: SUMMARY

Now at the end, let's repeat the most important aspects of this law: the person who resists the events of his/her life (by running away or fighting) will certainly face a lot of obstacles in the future, a lot of problems, a lot of negative circumstances. In life, when you are focused on a goal, you begin to see solutions, but when you take your eyes off the goal, you start to see problems. Resistance keeps you connected with problems.

Therefore, the Law of Least Resistance means diminishing the resistance with which you oppose life, so that your emotional attention remains focused towards solutions and results.

LAW 5: LAW OF VISUALIZATION

PART 1: SCIENTIFIC DESCRIPTION OF THE LAW

I'll start with a promise: from the beginning of this law I promise to create clarity in your mind once and for all, on the way to apply visualization correctly. In the last five years, I have tested several methods of visualization to reach a deep understanding of how these processes should be applied correctly. All of the knowledge that I gained over time on the processes of visualization, I will present synthesized within this law.

Here is a question to begin with:
"Why does materialization of what you want involves visualization processes?" Anyone who has exceeded the beginner level in using this concept of attraction should already know that the correct application of this law involves visualization processes. To be more specific, the correct application of this law involves associated visualization processes, but I will detail this process later.

What are these processes of visualization? They are the mental training periods in which you educate your subconscious concerning what you really want, specifically impregnating the subconscious with the mental images of what you want to materialize in your life as much clarity as possible.

The reason for this is that your subconscious does not know the difference between imagination and reality, and what you attract in the physical plane is in fact what governs your subconscious mind, as it represents about 90% of your mental potential. You do not attract what governs your conscious mind. You attract what governs your subconscious mind, which cannot differentiate between imagination and reality. It does not think, it just accepts unconditionally any image you place inside it. This is precisely why visualization processes are used to reprogram the subconscious.

When you frequently allow mental images of what you want in your mind, the older images lose their clarity in your subconscious mind, while new images begin to become clearer and they increasingly begin to crystallize more powerfully. So, you reprogram your consciousness.

On the other hand, when your mind is governed by the images of what you do not want, it goes into a paralyzed state of creation, that no longer has the power to materialize the things you wish for, because your mental programs refer to the polarity opposite of what you want. Furthermore, this state of mind blocks the physical action, thus blocking the results.

Since the subconscious is about 90% of your mental potential, naturally what you attract into your life depends mostly on your subconscious mind. So how you program the subconscious mind will elevate or lower you in life. It's like getting into an elevator. Regardless of the button you press, you have only two options: either climb or descend. Same with your mind: if you schedule it with negative thoughts, you go down permanently. But the polar opposite of this idea is true: you get great results only when your mind is governed by positive thoughts. What is inside you, will materialize out. What comes to you is totally attracted by you, usually subconsciously.

Through the process of visualization, you reprogram your mental computer, but for this it must see as clearly as possible the image of your materialization object. When you repeatedly visualize in your mental plane the image of your materialization object, you actually crystallize subconsciously more strongly what you will attract into your life. So, you reprogram your subconscious towards the object of your attraction.

*"Imagination is everything.
Is the power of prediction of what will follow in life."*
Albert Einstein

Visualization must be accompanied by a strong emotional load, is an experience full of emotions that makes you feel a state of emotional release, as you've already got what you want. It is a mental and emotional transposition into the state that you've already got what you want.

Next I will reveal to you the key of the visualization processes: the greatest secret of visualization processes is to draw mentally and emotionally that moment in the future (when you've got what you want) NOW, today. I will give you a very simple experience that will help you understand correctly what means to mentally and emotionally draw the future into the present.

Here is the process:

Step 1: Close your eyes and set in the room where you are, a point that you associate with the present moment.

Step 2: Set in your mind, another point that you associate with time in the future when you've already got what you want. Set the object of your attraction, mentally and emotionally, at this point.

Step 3: Mentally draw a line between the two points that we will call the timeline.

Step 4: Furthermore, you should reduce the line at a point where the future and the present are identified, become one so that your emotional states for the two points in time confuse between them. You mentally draw the emotional image from the future into the present and identify yourself with this condition. Keep this emotional state throughout the visualization, identify yourself with it, become that state that must live emotionally in you. This is the correct associated visualization process when you live the future with maximum intensity, but in the present moment, *NOW*. You become "that moment" living the joy of "*now*" and "*here*".

Let us venture further into the mental clarification of this law. When impregnating the mental images of what you want into your subconscious, it will set inside you the mental, emotional and physical resources that you need to accomplish your objective. These are inner resources, but your goal needs external resources because you do not live isolated in space, you interact in a system. Here comes the Universe's contribution by those resonant frequencies it creates with your thoughts.

Here is the process: it is very important to understand that the Universe does not give you what you want. It just holds the opportunities, people, events, circumstances around you, it offers only the tool by which what you place in your subconscious, becomes your reality by the power of your firmly focused thinking. Therefore, your thought is creative.

You see, emotion attached to your thought is the cause that triggers the process of materialization, and what you actually materialize is the effect of images you placed in your mind. We are talking about the Law of Cause – Effect. The reality is that an effect cannot occur without a cause behind.

We are all connoisseurs of the *Law of Cause – Effect*. We've all heard:

"Keep on knocking and the door will be opened to you! Keep on asking and you will receive what you asked for! Keep on seeking and you will find!"[10]

Of course it depends how you knock to open, how you ask to be given and how you look for to find and that is why you read these laws to understand the secrets of the materialization process from the right perspective. So, your emotional mind is the cause and what you materialize is the effect. Thus, you become creator just by the power of your thinking.

Let's also consider what happens if you do not follow the associated visualizing processes. In this situation, your mind sees only what you have or what you are now and therefore you will attract into your life more of what you have. You will not be too far away from the present results.

If you want different results, your mind must see different pictures and your emotions must strongly support these images. That's why lack of visualization keeps you trapped within the boundaries of the results that you have achieved so far. So, you're at the stage where you have a clarified mind as to why materialization involves associated visualization processes.

---
[10]*Orthodox bible*, Matthew, chapter 7

Now we move forward, and I will provide information on the correct way of application of the visualization processes. The quality and depth of information that you will find further will help you qualify within the professionals regarding the correct way of application of mental visualization processes. I recommend that you pay attention to what follows, as strategies of this process are extremely important ideas in the visualization process and you probably have not seen them before in such a clear manner.

First, it is essential to reveal some conditions that you must follow in the application of the visualization processes:

- Periods of mental training must take place for at least for 21-29 days. I recommend at least 30 days to you, but the process can continue until materialization of the object of your desire.

- Training is done daily, and if possible, I recommend that you make it about the same time each day, as the subconscious self-schedules efficiently. If you fail to work one day, you will have to prolong the process by another week. If you omit two days, then you have to restart the whole process.

Here are the concrete steps of the visualization process:

Step 1: Energy Balancing

This step is important as it prepares your mind for the materialization process. Here is how to apply it: before planting the image of the materialization object in your thinking garden, you must first cleanse the mental field because otherwise, you plant in a field full of weeds (negative thoughts, stress, dissatisfaction, frustration), specifically, low-frequency thoughts, as known in the specialized literature.

What is this cleansing practically: you must be reconciled with yourself, in full harmony with what you are and what you have right now. Basically, in this step, you clean at energetic level the low-frequency vibrations, you prepare the foundation on which you will build the materialization process, a clean foundation, not loaded with low-frequency vibration. When you are under stress, the energy in your body is unbalanced, the body is in a state of alarm and you must exit this state, so that your body rebalances its energy, enters into a state of relaxation.

Specifically, how do you do this?
I offer you a simple application method, very powerful and handy. The method comprises two steps of application.

Phase 1: Sit in a more comfortable position on the sofa or in bed, with your eyes closed and concentrate on your breathing that must be as deep as possible. The mental internalization process is as follows: deep inspiration becomes increasingly colder and deep exhalation becomes increasingly hotter. When you inhale, you absorb positive energy from the Universe and when you exhale, you send positive energy into the Universe. Inhalation and exhalation should be deep and slow. Repeat this process several times until you feel a deep state of relaxation. Through this process, you basically relax your conscious mind.

Phase 2: Furthermore, in a state of relaxation, you will need to repeat aloud a sentence, while your mind is focused on every word you say. When you say aloud, emotion is magnified in your body. Here is the process: view on your mind display every word with letters of fire, then say them loudly. During this process, you must keep your eyes closed. Thus, you must repeat three times aloud a sentence, engraving each word with letters of fire on your mental screen:

> I .... (your name) ...., forgive myself,
> love myself and accept myself as I am.
> Thank you!

The words must be said slowly, one after another, with pauses between them (so to sat then in your mind) and must be strongly viewed with eyes closed. It is important to identify yourself with every word you utter, in order for it to be emotionally absorbed in the process. So let's summarize. So far all you have to do is:

01. relax your conscious mind;
02. repeat that phrase in a state of focus.

So far you've just prepared your mind for the creative process, you cleared it of low-frequency vibrations.

Step 2: Printing the intention on the mental plane
This step really has power, as from here the process of materialization starts, from establishing the intent. Materialization starts mentally and then manifests physically. Over 90% of the materialization process takes place mentally, as the mind is the one that dictates matter and not vice versa. Printing of intention is made through the associated visualization processes. I do not recommend dissociated visualization, as it is difficult to generate strong emotions in this state.

Associated visualization means that you are associated, you feel all sensations that accompany an experience, that means you are in the movie, you're the actor. It's like a theatrical play in which you are the main actor.

Dissociated visualization means when you are dissociated, you have feelings about a particular experience, like being in the room and watching a play in which you are the main character.

Here is what I recommend as a life lesson: create a habit of being associated to what you enjoy and dissociated to what you do not like, identify yourself with the feelings and experiences that create pleasure for you and get away mentally and emotionally from what you do not like. If you make it a habit, you will gain a strong state of emotional control. This technique is very simple, but very powerful. So, printing of intent is done by images you are viewing in associated state on the display of your mind. The visualization process by pictures can be achieved by three methods, which act differently in terms of effects generated:

Method 1: through static images, photo type.
Here is the process: with eyes closed access the images and try to visualize them as clearly as possible on your mental screen.

The disadvantage of this method: when visualizing, you allow for less accurate mental images to crystallize in your mind.
The advantage of this method: it internalizes the process as you view the images on your mental screen, you do not see them somewhere outside yourself on a display.

Method 2: also by static images, like photographs, but this time, visualization is made with eyes open by contemplating on a display, a monitor or a digital photo frame, of the same images as in method 1. We do not speak of a simple image viewing, but of a process of contemplation of images, like a state of trance! Scrolling images must be automatic every 5-10 seconds and I recommend you be in a dark room, to prevent entry of other additional elements into your field of view.

The disadvantage of this method: it externalizes the process as you view images on a screen and not within your mind.

The advantage of this method: it fixes your mind on concrete, stable elements, leaving no room for less accurate images.

I recommend that you combine both methods: first enter a process of contemplation of images on a display, thus externalizing the process, then view the images on the mental screen, internalizing the process.

From a neurological standpoint, the visualization processes will be completed and will impregnate more accurate images in the subconscious, and in terms of mental resonances, you will generate better accuracy of your object materialization.

Method 3: animated method (static and dynamic) in which you "animate" those images, you run them mentally and become part of them as in a movie. This is generally the most effective of all methods. Specifically it means to animate images: for example if you decide that your goal is to get EUR 500.000, animate this photo, specifically imagine that you look at your bank account and that amount is written, imagine that you count the money, or how you will spend it. You have to take care of two aspects in the process of animation:

01. same movie to be permanent;
02. the process must be done in associated condition.

Let's summarize: in step 2 (printing intention on a mental plane), you choose one of the three visualizing methods and run it for a minimum of one month. The process must be in associated state.

Step 3: The continuous wait
The process of materialization does not consist only of those associated visualization rounds. And this is extremely important to understand, because here most errors occur.

Here is the process: what you do most of the time dictates what you attract into your life. Visualization processes are only mental training periods, in which you clarify your mind about what you really want and practically activate the vibrations corresponding to your materialization object at a higher energy. They act as references, milestones along the path. But what you visualize and feel predominantly determine your consciousness, the attractiveness of things and events in your life.

The power of visualization processes is given by the fact they accelerate the process of materialization and help you clarify your mind about what you really want. However, visualization processes must be completed by a continuous standby. Otherwise, you will interrupt the production of materialization. Therefore, focus on your goal as often as possible, actively maintaining the creative process. The continued wait should be accompanied by strong emotions and great faith.

If you want to attract a certain thing, it is necessary to imagine yourself mentally and emotionally in the state in which you already have what you want. For example, if you want a car feel as if you already have that car NOW, you drive it, live the moment, be in associate status. You can only materialize future through the power of the present, so you are the mental architect of your own destiny by what you think predominately.

There are people who find it hard to impregnate mentally the idea that they already have what they want. If you are one of those people, I offer you a solution: in the visualization process, do not fix your attention on the ultimate goal, but mentally and emotionally get involved in the development of your results today until the materialization of your desire.

PART 2: PRACTICAL TOOL FOR LAW APPLICATION

Under this law, I will provide you two practical application tools. The first tool refers only to periods of mental training in which you clarify your mind about what you really want. The second tool corresponds to what you do most of your time.
The materialization process has force only by applying both tools and here is why:

- the first tool sets your check points, references along the way, it clears your mind of what you want to materialize;

- the second tool helps you get from one terminal to the next, namely, acts between check points.

So let's start:

Tool 1: to be applied during periods of mental training

Before applying this process, you have to look for or build images of what you want to materialize. These photos must be on a display or a digital photo frame. I suggest you print them out and then put them in a presentation folder in which you look daily. This tool will be adapted exactly to the three steps of the visualization of which we discussed.

- Step 1: Balancing energy

Step 1: Get a more comfortable position on the sofa or in bed with eyes closed and concentrate on your breathing that must be as deep as possible. Breathe deeply and slowly as you inhale positive energy from the Universe. Exhale deeply and slowly while sending positive energy into the Universe. Repeat this process several times until you feel a deep state of relaxation.

Step 2: Furthermore, in a state of relaxation, with your eyes closed, visualize with letters of fire on the screen of your mind, every word then pronounce it aloud:

I, ... *(your name)* ... forgive myself, I love myself and accept myself as I am. Thank you!
Repeat the process 3 times.

- Step 2: Printing the intention on the mental plane

This is to view in associated condition the photos you took by the three methods.

Method 1: through images, photo type.
Here is the process: with your eyes closed try to access the images and clearly visualize them on your mental screen.

Method 2: through images, photo type, but this time, visualization is done with opened eyes, by contemplating them on a display, a monitor or a digital photo frame.

Method 3: Animated method (static and dynamic) when you "*animate*" these images, run them mentally and become part of them as a movie.

- Step 3: Continuous wait

For the materialization process to become as easy as possible for you to apply, step 3 is actually the application of the second tool in the materialization process.

Tool 2: to be implemented most of the time

This tool is to apply mind games as creative as possible for you, in which you have to get involved emotionally. Under this tool I will discuss a common topic for people: money. I will teach you how to print your subconscious with the idea of money, the idea of prosperity. This tool can be applied to any aspect of your life: home, relationships, car, health, etc. These mind games will change your level of consciousness towards money and then you will attract circumstances where the money will come to you. First, we have to question the scientific basis that greatly facilitates the application of this tool, and by the end I will present the mind games. It's very simple, you will be convinced immediately.

Let's start with the scientific base. Since the subconscious is what dictates your results, and it does not know the difference between imagination and reality, it means that you have a very powerful tool that you can use. This tool is your imagination. You'll never get out of poverty if you do not constantly practice the process of imagination. Prosperity can be acquired only after you print an image of wealth on your mental screen. Without strongly planting in your consciousness those images and emotions, prosperity will not materialize in your life. Remember that prosperity begins in your mind and then manifests on the physical plane. The money will come to you only when you will not miss it. As long you feel the lack of money, it will stay away from you, as what lacks is the reality of your mind, which then you manifest in the physical plane.

For the materialization of money to become easier for you and your subconscious mind to better integrate the mental state of prosperity, I recommend that you consider money as a stream of energy flowing through you. Let us say again, because it is very important: consider money as a stream of energy flowing through you. This process is very fair, because prosperity is first installed on a mental, emotional and energy plane and then manifests on the physical plane.

This technique, to consider money as a stream of energy flowing through you, reprograms easier your prosperity consciousness because when you focus on money, as an outside element, you emotionally place money somewhere outside you, in the exterior. If you do this association, which considers money as a stream of energy that flows through you, then you place the idea of money within you, as a part of you. When you internalize the process, the force of attraction is greater. When you externalize the process, the force of attraction is lower. The more you want more money, the energy flowing through you, should be higher. This mental game will entail an increase in the energetic levels towards money. Increased vibration leads on to higher levels of consciousness toward money and then you will attract people, circumstances, opportunities, through which money will come to you.

This association has power to materialize and that is why I recommend internalizing the mental process. Otherwise, you will encounter great difficulties in obtaining money, since you permanently place it somewhere outside you. There will be challenges anyway, since money does not fall from the sky, but by using the right tools, you can significantly reduce the size of the challenges and how to answer them. If your action is reduced to a state of faith that the Universe, for your sake, will trip and in its fall will lose money in your bag, well you're wrong, because it will not happen ever! I know there are materials in which you are told:

"Write on a piece of paper how much money you want and wear it with you for a year, and after a year you will be surprised to realize that the money really exists."

Let me tell you the truth: these are just absurd stories. If it were so easy to get money, then we all would have in pockets papers with wishes and we all would become extremely rich.

Below I will provide, as I promised, some mind games through which you will be able to impregnate your subconscious with the idea of prosperity, so as to acquire the prosperity consciousness. But you can be even more creative in generating mental games. Here are some examples that you can apply anywhere, anytime, under any conditions:

- When paying bills, imagine the money you give will come back to you twice more.

- When you take out money from the card, imagine that your account will get five times more money. Write on your card with a marker: X (times) 5.

- Put some money in your wallet that you do not spend. Put EUR 50 or EUR 100 or another amount depending on your possibilities. Every time you open the wallet you will see that amount of money, and it will change the state even when you pull the money out of your wallet. That amount that you do not spend, will maintain a state of good vibration regarding the money, it will help you feel more comfortable with the idea of money.

- Write every day on a sheet, "Money and I live in harmony". This money (write the sum) is already mine since I began the process of its materialization. Money comes to me:

- When you walk, imagine how you step on money, generate the feeling of financial security;

- Imagine your bank account daily loading with more money;

- Get yourself a notebook in which at least one day write a sentence related to the harmony between you and money;

- Imagine that all money in the world is the property of people, and you have the right to more and more money, as you know and apply the laws that govern prosperity and success.

In the end, remember the following idea: consider money as an energy stream that flows through you so that your subconscious integrates the idea of money more easily.

PART 3: SUMMARY

Visualization refers to printing on your mental screen, in associated state, the images that match your attraction object (what you want to materialize). This visualization process should be done frequently, day after day, maximum intensity being recorded during periods of mental training.

Let's recall the concrete steps of the visualization process:

- *Step 1:* Balancing energy – when you have to repeat a phrase in a state of focus:

    I, ... (your name) ...forgive myself,
    I love myself and accept myself as I am.
    Thank you!

- *Step 2:* Printing the intention mentally

Here there are 3 ways:

Method 1: Using images, photo type – by viewing on your mental screen;

Method 2: Using images, photo type – by the contemplation of images on a display;

Method 3: Animated method (static and dynamic) when you "animate" those images, run them mentally and become part of them as a movie.

- *Step 3:* The continuous wait – is a state accompanied by strong emotions and great faith. You must keep this state active until the materialization of what you want.

LAW 6: LAW OF GRATITUDE

PART 1: SPIRITUAL DESCRIPTION OF THE LAW

Here is what the Law of Gratitude states: Be grateful for what you have now and what you are now, but be focused on growing.

I'll start this law through a very touching and suggestive story about the feeling of gratitude. Here is the story:

"There was once a poor young man. He was so poor that he wore torn clothes and he did not have anything to eat. And one day, he was so hungry that he decided to knock on a door to ask for something to eat, because he had no money. He went to a house, knocked on the door and a very beautiful woman opened it. Feeling ashamed, he asked the woman for a glass of water. But she realized that he was hungry and brought him a large glass of milk. The young man drunk it and finally asked her how much he owes although he had no money, but she said he did owe her anything. Then he thanked her and left.

After 12 years, he became a very famous doctor with a lot of money. The woman who gave him the glass of milk became very ill and was hospitalized. After many efforts, the doctors managed to save her, and when healed, a doctor brought an envelope with all her hospitalization expenses. The woman knew that these costs would be very high and she would have to work her whole life to be able to pay. She did not even have the courage to open the envelope, but eventually did so, and on the sheet were written these words:

"Fully paid long ago, with a large glass of milk."[11]

Here is what I want to tell you: beware how you touch peoples' souls, as in the long-term, you will get exactly what is in your soul. What you do to others, will come back to you. Gratitude is a feeling that you must live continuously and you have to identify with it.

"He who is not satisfied with what he has, would not be satisfied even with what he would like now to have."
Socrates

This lesson focuses in it the meaning of the Law of Gratitude. You may think your life is so disastrous that you do not have reasons to be thankful!

But I tell you, think about this:
"How would it be to not have hands?"
"Imagine that your legs are paralyzed!"
"What if you have a loved one in a wheelchair for life?"

Still looking for reasons to be ungrateful?
I think you have enough reasons to be thankful, regardless of where you are right now. The most obvious indicator of a little soul is ingratitude. The most obvious indicator of a great soul is the attitude of gratitude constantly manifested. Gratitude enriches all things in your life.

Here is the great challenge in the Law of Gratitude: you have to be grateful when you do not have what you want. If you do not know how to be grateful when you have nothing, you will not be grateful even when you have everything.

---

[11]Dr. Kelly, Howard - A glass of milk, www.povesticutalc.ro

You're not grateful to God just when you have what you want. Status of gratitude must be manifested in your consciousness even when you do not have what you want. You cannot declare peace and gratitude to God only when good things manifest in your life, and declare war and lack of gratitude when bad things occur in your life. Do not make God responsible for your results.

If you are two days in the desert and you are thirsty, then someone gave you a cup of water, then you should be grateful for that cup of water. But now that you have all the water you want, you do not show gratitude. If you were a homeless man and you were shivering, and someone gave you clothing, then you become grateful. But now, because you have clothes and a place to sleep, you do not manifest a state of gratitude. If you had a serious illness and you are saved, you would be extremely grateful that you were saved. But now, you're not really grateful for your health.

So be constantly grateful for what you have and what you are, and this continued state of gratitude will generate vibrations that will attract more things for which to become grateful. One who has a continued state of gratitude, will receive other things for which to be grateful.

So be thankful now and at any time of day, for all the good things in your life, be grateful for the water you drink, for the bed where you sleep, for the job you have, for your health, for the car, for the opportunities in your life. Be grateful for your power of materialization, be thankful for everyday food, for people around you, for achievements in your life, for this book you are reading. Be grateful now, and tomorrow will bring many things for which you should manifest gratitude in your life.

When you live in gratitude, you will attract more strongly similar energies, which will materialize more experiences and more things for which you become grateful, so you'll be creating the circumstances to materialize what you really want.

When you manifest the feeling of gratitude, you virtually reorient yourself vibrationally to the good things in your life, and this vibrational shift will create further conditions that would attract to you more things for which to become grateful. But it is impossible to attract more good things into your life, if you emit a feeling of lack of gratitude for what you have and for what you are right now. If in the present moment you emit thoughts expressing ingratitude, basically you create circumstances that will materialize exactly what you do not want in your future.

In the materialization process, it does not matter if you think about the past, present or future. The moment at which you think has absolutely no significance in materialization, because you actually generate the thought in the present, "*NOW*". You transmit vibration in the present moment. If you think about a negative event from the past, you generate the thought in the present and virtually you will materialize in your future exactly those negative things that govern your mind. Thus, you will lock abundance even mentally, and what you attract into your future are events that are not in fact what you want.

So be thankful "*NOW*" at any time of the day, for what you have and what you are, and that will attract what you want in your future. Gratitude has the power to change your life, because you basically put yourself in a high frequency vibration that attracts good things.

The materialization of the future is done only by the power of the present, and you already know this. So, if you are ungrateful, today, practically this is what you will reap in the future. So lack of gratitude will manifest in the personal area, professional area, financial area, virtually all aspects of your life.

You can say that now you are unhappy because of the circumstances in your life and that you will become happy when you get what you want (dream house, favorite car, EUR 100,000 or the loved one). And I say that in the best case, assuming you get the things you wish for, you'll be happy, but briefly, whereas when you materialize what you wanted, you already look ahead again in the future and you will enter into a state of unhappiness until the next objective.

Suppose you are focused on your goals and achieve them! In this situation, your happiness will be reduced to only those times when you've reached your goals. And between those objectives, unhappiness will dominate.

Now I ask you:

" Continuing in this manner for ten years or twenty, or thirty years do you think you'll be able to declare yourself happy?"

Of course not! You will only have a long road full of problems and unhappiness among which moments of happiness were occasionally occurring. You cannot be happy while you're in search of happiness, because you mentally place happiness on your timeline somewhere ahead of you in the future and as long as you continue to be in the pursuit of happiness, it will remain as far, because again, you placed it ahead you in the future as far as possible. If you want to be happy, you must place the happiness just now: happiness is here, now, at this moment, it is manifested by the power of present. It knows no other location in time as when you think about happiness, you do an assessment of it right in this moment. Therefore, its power is manifested through you, now and here, right now.

So turn off the light of yesterday and live now because you are the creator of your own destiny. It has always been so! Wherever you try to place the happiness on your timeline, past or future, you cannot talk about happiness, but an illusion of happiness. It's just up to you if you choose to use your present misery to go in the future, but it will generate further unhappiness, because in fact, you planted that in your mind. You reap what you sow. It's a law!

As a conclusion, the only way to get happiness and gratitude in the future is currently living through a sense of gratitude. Gratitude redirects your thoughts and emotions and creates the optimal conditions for you in the future. When you are grateful and thankful for the present, the next moment will bring reward. Remember a powerful lesson: be grateful for what you have now and what you are, but be focused on growing.

Strong and constant gratitude keeps you connected to the source of creation and materializes the opportunities through which your dreams manifest in your life. Lack of gratitude breaks the link with the source of creation and blocks the emergence of opportunities in your life. If you do not know where to start the process of changing your inner vibration, then begin with gratitude, as it is one of the most powerful tools that redirects your energy toward what you want. Do this regularly every day until you feel filled with gratitude and reach a sense of inner peace. Whenever your inner state is not right, write down the things you feel grateful for. Within minutes your inner state will change, because where your thoughts are, there your emotional energy will be.

Metaphorically speaking, if you associate darkness with ingratitude, and express gratitude with light, when it is dark inside you simply turn on the light. If you focus on the dark, there will be no light. You won't change your inner state identifying yourself with what you do not want, as this action will create conditions that would attract more of what you do not want. If you want a different status, then turn on the light of gratitude.

Write the things for which you are grateful. Change your vibration and you will change the conditions of appearance in your life what you want. If your feelings of gratitude are small, the results you will attract will also be small. If your feelings of gratitude are great, the results you'll attract will also be higher. Therefore, the size of what will materialize will be the measure of your feelings of gratitude. You cannot attract great results without gratitude in your life. There is a cause and an effect: the effect is the results of your life, the cause is the feeling of gratitude.

PART 2: PRACTICAL TOOL FOR LAW APPLICATION

I'll give you two tools, very easy to apply and with a great deal of change in your life. I recommend that you use them both.

Tool 1: Transmission of thoughts of gratitude

Whenever you feel a negative state, choose a person to convey your thoughts of gratitude, appreciation to.

You can even choose a person you do not like, as the people hardest for you to love are those who have the greatest need, because they put you in difficulty and in your attempt to deal with the situation you will be pushed towards development. So express your gratitude to a person and you'll find two reactions, both beneficial:

01. first, this action will change your mood, from a negative to a positive one;

02. thoughts that you have sent to that person, you will find returned to you, from the same person or from others.

When this process becomes a habit in your life, you will have clear proof that what leaves from you returns to you because you're the generating source of all events that manifest in your life.

Tool 2: Be grateful in this moment

To express your gratitude that attracts the circumstances through which you materialize what you want to you, I recommend that you buy a book of gratitude. The book of gratitude has unwritten pages, as these pages are yours. Inside the book, you'll be able to express your gratitude both in the present moment and your intentions of gratitude for what you want to achieve. I'll give you two concrete examples taken from my book of gratitude.

Example 1: Intentions of Gratitude: EUR 1,000,000.
I am really grateful NOW because money is already present. This money is the reward for services that I can offer.
From this moment I do not think about how much I want to win, but I get involved physically, emotionally and

intellectually in performing the necessary services to attract this money.

Thank you by gratitude,
28.06.2010

Example 2: Gratitude NOW: perfect health.
I thank NOW the divine creative power for my perfect health. I feel increasingly better from day to day.

Thank you by the magnetic force of the heart,
25.06.2012

PART 3: SUMMARY

Here is what the Law of Gratitude states: Be grateful for what you have now and what you are now, but be focused on growing.

In the process of materialization, it does not matter if you think about the past, present or future. The moment about which you think has absolutely no significance in the matter, because you actually generate the thought in the present, "NOW". You transmit vibration in the present moment. So the only way to get happiness and gratitude in the future is to live with a sense of gratitude today.

LAW 7: LAW OF FORGIVENESS

PART 1: SPIRITUAL DESCRIPTION OF THE LAW

First, I will give a human face to this law, then we will analyze it at the spiritual level. Therefore, from the beginning, this is the human face: the story of the orange box.

"One sunny afternoon of August, a wise teacher came into class with lots of cardboard boxes and placed amidst his students, and he said the following: this is your assignment for next week.

For starters, here is what to do: each of you choose your preferred cardboard box. After each student had chosen a box, the teacher approached one of the students and said the following: "for each person who upset you and you decided not to forgive, you must add one orange to the box. And to know to whom that orange belongs, you'll stick a label with the name of that person. For one week you will be carrying the box with you at home, in the car, when you do your homework, in the city, even at night you will keep the box at the foot of your bed. And in any case you must not give up your box of oranges. So must each of you do".

Students, at first, were amused by this strange assignment, but immediately went to work: each started with great ardor to add oranges labeled with the names of persons they could not forgive.

Thus, students had added lots of oranges to their boxes with the names of those who had upset them from childhood to the present. As the days passed, students added more oranges with the names of people who upset them in the past whose behavior they felt was inexcusable. However, they began to realize that from day to day, the box became increasingly heavy.

Oranges placed at the beginning of the week, already spoiled and had a disgusting smell and damage was expanding faster and faster to the other oranges. But the biggest problem was that they each had the responsibility to carry the box to the stores, the bus, the restaurant, to dates, to table, to school.

So their task became increasingly difficult as the cardboard boxes were breaking increasingly more and a sticky and smelly liquid was already running out of the boxes. With great difficulty, the students were able to cope with the load they had.

After a week, the students met again with the teacher and began to tell him how difficult their task was.

At the end of the lesson, the teacher approached a student and said the following:
"That box you had with you everywhere and which was so difficult to carry, is the symbol of the spiritual weight you carry with you when you gather your hate, envy, unforgiveness toward others. If you'd had forgiven those people from the beginning, then your box would be empty. When you forgive someone, you actually do a favor to yourself".[12]

Here is the wisdom that this story brings to the surface: forgiveness is a benefit for you firstly, since you're the one who frees your soul from the heavy burden to bear.

---
[12]The story of the orange box, www.povesticutalc.ro

And now let me ask you, the reader:

"In your box, how many oranges can you collect in a week from today and what are you going to do with them?" Give yourself an answer.

Let's talk further about the components of this law. The Law of Forgiveness has two components:

The first component of the Law of Forgiveness refers to the forgiveness of others

The story you just read I think is highly suggestive in this regard. Forgiving positions yourself emotionally in a high frequency.

"Why do you think, when you forgive someone, you feel a state of emotional relief? Do you think it is coincidence?"

Of course not! What you are doing at the time, is that you let go of that negative energy load that you had with you. And to make myself better understood, I will tell you another story:

"A teacher taught his students about the importance of the release of negative emotions! And this is what he did: he took a glass of water and walked around the room quietly. A minute had passed, then five minutes, ten minutes, but the teacher was still walking through the room. All students looked at him in silence and waited, but without understanding the message. After fifteen minutes he stopped, raised his glass in front of them and pulled from his pocket a € 100 bill, and said:

"Who knows how heavy this glass of water is, gains €100".

Students were quick to respond precisely, saying the glass is 200 ml, 300 ml, 275 ml, 250 ml.

Having listened to all, the teacher told them the following:

"Its absolute weight does not matter. It matters how

long you hold it up: one minute – no problem, an hour – you will hurt your arm, one day – the entire hand will be paralyzed."[13]

In any of the 3 cases, the weight of the glass of water has not changed. What changed was only time, and the longer you hold the glass in hand, the heavier it will become. It is the same for emotions in your body, stress, worries in your life, they are like the glass of water:

- if you think about them a minute, nothing happens;
- if you think about them longer, your soul begins to hurt;
- if you think about them permanently, they paralyze your mental forces.

And until you let go of those emotions that pull you down and drain your power, until you give them away, they exist within you.

What is the moral of this story: if you want to get rid of the emotional burden of the past, then don't keep it with you overnight. And now I want to ask you:
"How empty is your glass in the day to come?"

The second component of the Law of Forgiveness refers to forgiveness of yourself

Surely, in your past you did wrong things. Of course you've done them with the consciousness you had at that time. Here is the problem: if you do not forgive the wrong things in your past, that means you have to take them with you in the future, day after day, year after year.

---
[13] Unknown author

The secret lies in forgiveness. Liberate yourself from that emotional burden. Forgive and let negative thoughts pass, while you focus your attention towards thoughts that give you power. See, what happens when you forgive yourself and forgive someone else, is that you let go of your past resentments and thus rebalance your body's energetic system. And then, the energy will begin to flow freely through your body and your mind will move from a locked state to a state of release and creativity.

Let us further analyze the influence of forgiveness in the spiritual, energetic, physical and mental planes.

01. Forgiveness (spiritually) helps you be in a much better connection with divinity.

Why is it important?
Divinity is the source from which you get good ideas, creativity, and inspiration.

02. Forgiveness (in terms of energy) helps to diminish or even eliminate some of the energetic imbalances of your system.

Why is it important?
The cause of all events in the physical plane (health status, disease, money, relationships, practically everything is manifested in your life), you will find it in fact at the energetic and spiritual level.

03. Forgiveness (physical plane) helps you maintain health, because thoughts are the cause of diseases.

Why is it important?
We really do not need to provide any justification here.

04. Forgiveness (mental plane) helps you change your focus direction from what you do not want and the emotional load to what you really want.

Why is it important?
Focus points you physically, emotionally, intellectually, to what is truly important to you,
basically directs you to the results.

PART 2: PRACTICAL TOOL FOR LAW APPLICATION

I will give you below a very simple technique to apply to relieve your heavy load to bear due to lack of forgiveness and hence the negative thoughts from your mind. Be careful:

Step 1: Imagine the sky with two types of clouds: some dark and some light.

Step 2: Mentally create the following combination: the sky is your mind, and the clouds are your thoughts.

Step 3: All you have to do is just focus on the clouds. This is how it is done specifically:

- every time you think about an event or a negative situation and put emotional load in the process, what you do is identify yourself with a dark cloud in the sky, corresponding to your negative focus;

- on the other hand, every time you think about a positive event or situation and put emotional load in the process, what you do is identify yourself with a bright cloud in the sky, corresponding to your positive focus.

What you do in both cases is deliberately identify yourself with a cloud in the sky, focusing on it, giving it your whole mental and emotional attention. Here is the reality: you're not a cloud, you are the sky. Your mind is the sky. In the sky there are a lot of clouds, just as your mind is governed by a lot of thoughts. If you identify with storm clouds, well this is simply your deliberate decision, but it is the truth of your mind analyzed in a proper perspective.

Clouds appear and then disappear, they come and go, their condition of existence is passing. Now here is the question for you:

"Who neither appears, nor disappears, nor remains, nor goes?" I think you already know the answer.

So, who neither appears, nor disappears, nor remains, but neither leaves is the sky. It was, is and will still be there.

Think that from tomorrow the sky says: I chose to go! Could you picture this? If it leaves, who would take its place: a picture, a great emptiness, a reflection of the world? Can you imagine that? So no matter what happens to the clouds, they come and go but the sky remains. It is the same with your mind. It does not go away. It was, is and will be there. Your thoughts are fleeting instead. Only they come and go.

So, when those dark storm clouds appear on your mind's sky, simply change your direction of focus on light clouds, the positive thoughts. Basically, in this way you will feed your mind with positive thoughts and you'll starve the negative thoughts, which from lack of food will become smaller and smaller until they no longer have any power over you.

This tool helps you look at the unpleasant events in your life from a detached perspective and full of wisdom. Applied frequently, this extremely simple tool has the power to produce very big changes on the focusing direction of your predominant thoughts.

PART 3: SUMMARY

Here is a definition of forgiveness: forgive and let negative thoughts pass, while you maintain focused your attention towards thoughts that give you power.

The Law of Forgiveness has two components:

01. forgiveness of yourself;
02. forgiveness of others.

Forgiveness is a gain for you first, since you're the one who frees the soul from the heavy burden to bear.

LAW 8: LAW OF GIVING

PART 1: SPIRITUAL DESCRIPTION OF THE LAW

Put simply, this is what the law says: give to receive! As a metaphorical representation of how this law is manifesting in your life, imagine a pendulum in motion. Associate the left side of the pendulum with the idea of "giving" and the right side with the idea of "receiving". The harder you push the pendulum to the left, the further it will swing to the right. This law acts similarly in your life: as the size of your gift is greater, the more you will get in return. When you stop "giving", you stop "receiving".

For a precise picture of how you applied this law to your past, it is enough to make an assessment of the present moment. If what you get now is negative, this is an indicator that accurately confirms your past, what you gave was negative. I know this is not news that you enjoy. But, here is the good news: what you will receive in the future is determined by what you give right in this moment. Now, you have the opportunity to reshape the image of your future depending on the size of your gift. And how you decide, so be it! Let's see what are the important aspects of this law:

The first important aspect of the law: The sequence

The sequence refers to taking a first step and then moving to on to the second one. It is like the law of cause and effect, which states there can be no effect without first existing a cause. Therefore, the process is as follows: First the cause is generated and then the effect occurs.

So it is with the Law of Giving, which has two major phases:

Step 1: refers to the concept of "*giving*";
Step 2: refers to the concept of "*receiving*".

The law states "Give to Receive!"
This means that before you receive, you must first give.
If you do not respect the sequence of the law, this means that you first want to accumulate enough and then to give, you want to receive without first offering. But, what starts from the source returns to the source, what leaves from you returns to you, because you are the source of creation by the way you think. Your thought is creative and materializes physically. If nothing left from you, then you will not get anything in return. Think:

"How do you want to harvest if you have not first planted?"
"How do you want to get if you have not given first?"

If you have negative thoughts towards a person, who is the one who thinks negatively? Who is activating mentally and emotionally the image of negativity? It is actually you, who think negatively and not the other person. You cannot hurt anyone by thinking, without this hurting you too. So it is with positive thinking. When you generate positive thoughts towards a person, who delivers those thoughts? You're the one that has those thoughts. Therefore, those thoughts actually position you in a positive vibration that attracts similar situations, since this is actually what you emit. Moving on!

The second important aspect of the law: The offer

The law does not say what to offer. You can give money, information, love, material things, virtually anything you have. Here is what you need to understand clearly about the offer: you cannot work with this law by trying to make an exchange, because it does not matter what you give and how much you give, what matters is the vibration in which you are when giving, specifically, you must give from the desire of giving. You do not have to give like making an exchange, as correct operation of the law is subject to the spiritual power that you attach to the action of giving.

> *"It's not how much we give but
> how much love we put into giving."*
> Mother Teresa

The third important aspect of the law: The location

The great challenge when you want to give is the location, specifically to whom you give. You should not give to just anyone, because what is given by you, should grow. It is like a seed planted in the ground. For the seed to grow, it should be planted on fertile ground. If you plant on infertile ground, then the seed will not grow or thrive, and in these conditions what do you think you'll get back? Nothing!

So, you give from the desire to give, but you have to give only to those who will produce results with what you offered. Otherwise, it's like trying to do good to a person, but by force. You can coerce people, but you will never help by force, as the desire for change and growth must come from them. From you, can only come the wish to help. But you cannot help the one who does not help himself. Therefore, if you try to help forcefully, you lose the vibration, and lower yourself energetically and spiritually. The three issues that we have discussed so far refer to the concept of "giving". Let's remember these three important aspects:

The first aspect: The sequence (first give and then expect to receive).

The second aspect: The offer (offer what you have in abundance).

The third aspect: The location (specifically to whom you give, because you have to only give to those who will produce results with what you offered).

Next, we approach the second concept of this law: The concept of *"receiving."* A big mistake many make is that they give and even put love in what they give, but they violate the second law, which is the concept of *"receiving"*. They give, but their mistake is that they do not expect to receive. It is true that *"receiving"* is subject to *"giving"*, but it is not sufficient, because you have to be in the mental and emotional state of *"receiving"*.

So, to receive, you must put yourself in this situation, but you should not expect to receive from the same people to whom you gave. You just translate yourself mentally and emotionally to a state of receiving, but do not set the way in which to receive or the persons from whom to receive. This is not the responsibility of your mind. What comes to you, is because (as we discussed in other laws) of resonance frequencies. So do not force the Universe to bring you what you want in a way determined by you.

If you oppose the law and continue to do what you did in the past, then you will continue to receive what you received. Do not expect to do things in the same manner as before and to get different results, since the law is not working that way. So begin today to develop your correct mental setting to apply the law in your life.

"You must give as much as you want to receive. If you want a whole heart, give a whole lifetime."
Friedrich Ruckert

PART 2: PRACTICAL TOOL FOR LAW APPLICATION

All you have to do from today is to develop two habits:

01. The habit of giving from what you have (money, information, love, material things, etc.). Remember: you have to give from the desire of giving.

02. The habit of receiving (you must put yourself in the mental and emotional condition to receive).

So, make a lifestyle of this instrument, since by only giving from what you have, you can get what you want.

PART 3: SUMMARY

The Law of Giving states: Give to Receive!

Here are the important aspects of the concept of "*giving*":

- The sequence (first give and then expect to receive).
- The offer (offer what you have in abundance).
- The location (you should only give to those who will produce results with what you offered).

Here is the important aspect of the concept of "*receiving*": you should position yourself in the mental and emotional state of "*receiving*".

LAW 9: LAW OF VOID

PART 1: SPIRITUAL DESCRIPTION OF THIS LAW

In order to help you understand this law from a more correct perspective, I will begin by analyzing the events taking place both in you exterior plane and within your interior plane, whereas in psychological terms, the reality of your life has two components: one exterior and one interior.

Exterior:
- You have the habit of collecting things that you have not used for a long time, that you do not use and do not intend to use, but you still keep them, with the idea that in the future you may need them;

- You have the habit of repeating all sorts of activities with which you are familiar, but they do not get you results and satisfaction, thinking that without them your life would be empty;

- You have the habit of keeping relationships with people that do not bring you any progress.

Interior:
- You have the habit of retaining hate, sadness, fear, fights and all sorts of negative emotional states, all these referring to events belonging to your past.

Well, this wrong form of manifestation both in the exterior and interior plane applies to most people. Here is the essential part for you to understand: not the manifestation itself really interests us, but the effect it produces, specifically the outcome of this type of manifestation in your life. Therefore, here is the question:

"What is the result of such interior and exterior manifestation in your life?" What actually happens is that you keep captive in your body's energetic field, negative energetic vibrations and you block the emergence of new opportunities.

In order to work correctly with this law, you must remove as much as possible of what is useless in your life, both in the exterior and interior planes. This process of removing what is unimportant in your life creates an empty vacuum and this gap will be filled with what you want to materialize in your life. If you keep that load in the two planes, you will not create a gap, a vacuum, through which the good things enter into your life. You block thus the emergence of circumstances to materialize what you want. Therefore, to work in harmony with the Law of Void, it is necessary to create first the conditions by which what you want can enter into your life.

Here is a concrete example:

If you have decided to enter into a new relationship, what you need to do in order to work in harmony with the Law of Void, is to create an empty space, specifically, to disconnect completely from the old relationship. Disconnecting must take place in the two above-mentioned planes:

01. The interior plane – is the emotional foundation on which the old relationship was built.

Simply, no longer give conscious thought, think permanently about the future relationship, or think that it was simply an event from which you gained experience for a more adequate relationship. After all, to become good in relationships, in psychological terms, you must have had between 4 to 6 long-term relationships, otherwise, later there is a high probability you will make mistakes throwing your marriage on the rocks.

02. The exterior plane – that means you will never see that person again and not keep objects from that person around you.

The attitude of keeping these objects will mentally hamper the emergence of another person in your life, because this attitude of keeping, locks your mind in the memories of the past, and your predominant energy will be directed towards the past.

The Law of Void means to create a void, a space, and in this way, you create the conditions for the emergence of a new person in your life.

Next, pay attention to what follows, as the essence behind the action is the psychological part attached to the actions that you do in the two planes (exterior and interior). Basically, what hinders you in life are not the old objects that you keep around you, or relationships that do not bring any progress to you, but the mentality of stagnation that develops within your mind and programs your consciousness level. It is the mental setting attached to the action itself.

As a conclusion: if you really want to get something new, you have to start by creating a space, eliminating what keeps you glued to the spot both in the interior and exterior plane. Thus, the energy will flow freely through you, and this free flow will create the conditions for the emergence of new opportunities, people and things in your life.

PART 2: PRACTICAL INSTRUMENT OF LAW APPLICATION

I personally may not know you, but I respect our relationship and that is why I would like you to let me help you in applying the law. To do this, let's start a project together, which consists of two steps. Are you ready?

Step 1: Look around you and decide what things you do not use and clearly do not intend to use. Collect them all, then either give them to someone or throw them away. Jump to action as of today, do not delay, because if you delay, the chance to take action decreases ever more.

Step 2: Look into your life and write on a sheet of paper, who are the people who pull you down constantly. Write them out, it is not enough just to think about them. What you need to do is to get away from them, and if possible, to remove those people from your life. Of course you cannot get rid of all those who pull you down, but you will certainly significantly reduce the list of those who don't bring value in your life.

Therefore, change the insignificant people from your life with those who help you evolve constantly. If you do not find new people to replace those who pull you down, then I remind you the solution: replace them with people on CDs, talking about principles of materialization, attitude, leadership, dreams, the power of decisions, communication, emotional intelligence, principles of success, etc. You might become almost alone, but this is not serious, it is a new beginning, as you created a void that will enable the emergence of people that will help you in your process of development. Thus, in a few years, you'll be a person with a strong attitude, with completely different results, with a very good emotional control, and with a clear direction in life.

So, go to the mirror, look into your eyes and make the decision to clean up your life right now: both outside and inside you. Then move on to concrete action in this direction.

Do not wait for tomorrow, take action even in this moment, because tomorrow you may no longer do it, because your mind will begin to look for excuses! Postponing kills decision and action.

PART 3: SUMMARY

In order to work correctly with this law, you must remove what keeps you in place both from your interior and exterior planes. This process of removing unimportant things in your life creates an empty void and in this gap what you want to manifest will appear. Basically, this void creates the emergence of new opportunities, people and things in your life.

LAW 10: LAW OF THE ORGANIZED PLAN

PART 1: SCIENTIFIC DESCRIPTION OF THE LAW

Both, you and I, have reached the stage where we can look back at all the other nine universal laws of materialization that you need, in order to give life to the creative power in you. This last law, which I called the Law of the Organized Plan is basically an extension to other nine laws. The reason I chose to attach it to the Concept of Attraction is because most people make the most and the biggest mistakes exactly at this law.

Here is what you need to set clearly in your mind: all the other nine laws, in which we ventured together, have one goal: to help you create every possible condition in order to activate the energetic and spiritual forces underlying the materialization processes.

Therefore, the nine laws are practically nine keys with which you can unlock the energetic and spiritual channels through which the flow of abundance may come to you. However, opening the energetic and spiritual channels is not a sufficient condition to achieve results, because you have to act as well. Imagine an airplane. It needs both wings to fly.

So it is in your case: on the one hand, you must unlock the energetic and spiritual channels, and on the other hand, you have to take concrete action towards the objectives. If long-term persistence is added to these two conditions (in this context I mean years), you will achieve the results that will produce important changes in your life.

There are many people who have developed the following erroneous belief: if they pray, God, by His boundless goodness, will solve their problems. These are people who are always waiting for luck. Have you met any? But what is this word called luck and how does it manifests in your life? Luck is not something you stumble upon and suddenly your life takes a different picture. Luck is nothing but the intersection of skills and opportunity. Those who expect luck to manifest in their lives, are only dreaming and they should wake up. Remember that without your direct involvement, the Universe will not materialize what you want.

The Law of the Organized Plan puts a truth that I know in the spotlight and all who have reached success in life support it. So, here is what the Law of the Organized Plan states: to get what you want, you have to work in this direction. If you look at the surface, it is likely to have a tendency to say: good, but that's natural! I recommend to you that you not be hasty with this superficial analysis. The fact that most people make mistakes concerning just this law, is not at all an accident. The average man does not understand the application and operation of this Law from the proper perspective.

The Law states that in order to get what you want, you have to work in this direction. I didn't say just to work, but I said to work in this direction. We're talking about work directed, focused on results, following a strategy and a well-organized plan, since work without direction will hold you back! Everyone works, but only a small part of them plan their long-term work, using an organized plan that is practically your roadmap, oriented to achieve results.

I'll even give you a visual representation of what a roadmap means. If you need to go from city A to city B, and the distance is 400 km, to reach the destination, you need a guidance system, which in this case is represented by the road signs. Without signs, you won't get anywhere. So it is with your life. To get the results you desire in the future, you first need to define clearly and specifically what are those results, then you have to build a map, a strategic plan in time which will be your orientation tool, your GPS. In other words, you know where you are, you know where to go and you know what you have to do to get there. Most people have a GPS with a virus. They go in life, but without a long-term direction, they are defocused, their mind is full of negative thoughts, stress, frustration, react to what is happening in the external environment and permanently struggle with life.

Look at those who have little results in life. They are the people who work the most. On the other hand, look at those who have reached success. They work, but they allocate time for what is truly important in their lives. So both categories are working, but the difference lies in the results. While some obtain small results, some achieve fabulous results.

So what makes the difference? Here is the answer: those who have a hundred times more and have quality relationships and life, they do not work a hundred times more. But what do they do differently? Well, they think on a scale of one hundred fold. The difference is that they work following a well-organized plan and correctly apply the other nine laws in their lives. Do they do something different? In some cases, probably they do, but nothing that really has power in the process of obtaining happiness and success. And if you find my words pretentious, I assure you that when you make a lifestyle out of these ten laws, you will get to two clear conclusions:

01. your success depends on the level to which you manage to apply these ten laws;

02. almost all aspects of your life fall into the patterns of these laws.

When you get to this level of understanding, you may agree that you have taken control of your future forever. I respect those who have decided to change their lives and move to large-scale continuous action to produce a change. Of course, within this Law, I cannot present all the concepts related to Law of the Organized Plan, but I won't leave you without making available to you the most important aspects of it. So let's start:

01. What is your dream?

First, here is a story for the soul: The story of the wise!
"There was once in a village, a wise old man who had answers to all questions. And many people who needed learning came to him. And one day, two young men from the village wanted to make trouble for the wise man. And they said the following: we'll catch a bird, we'll go with it to the old man and ask if the bird we have in our hands is alive or dead. And if he says it's alive, then we will strangle the bird with our hands, and if he says it is dead, we will release the bird and it will fly.

They went to the old man and told him the following:
"If indeed you are so wise as everyone says, then tell us if this bird we hold in our hands is alive or dead? And the wise man answered to the one who asked:

- Young man, the life of that bird is in your hands."[14]

This is the whole story. So, your life is right in your hands, and you're the one who puts dreams inside it.

---
[14]Tracy, Brian. *The future depends on you: 12 key factors of the unlimited success*, Curtea Veche Publishing House, 2004

And you can give wings to your dreams and they will fly like a bird, or you can cut the wings of those dreams and they will disappear, and if they die, you will die too, because your life will be empty without dreams. So I ask:

"What is your dream?"

I want you to keep this question in your mind:

"What is your dream?"

You see, mental clarification of what you want is the first step in the process of change. You will never be able to get what you did not even define that you want to achieve. The problem of most people is that they do not define clearly and specifically what they really want. They do not even have dreams, they have desires that change from day to day depending on the circumstances of their lives.

02. Direction of Your Future

If you want to check the direction you're headed to in life in the next five years, it is sufficient to analyze what you did with your time in the last six months. This analysis is an indicator of accuracy. Think hard on what actions you have focused your attention, who are the people you interacted with, what did you do with your time? I recommend that you remember what you read below: you show your priorities in life depending on how you spend your time.

03. Think on paper

To achieve prosperity in life, your wealth consciousness must be extremely strong. You will not achieve prosperity by only thinking about it or having an interest which you occasionally manifest. Action must be continuous, large-scale, towards a well-defined objective. I recommend to clearly detail this great goal on paper in terms of action.

"All successful people think also on paper!"
Brian Tracy

The other people think only in their minds. They do not have the courage to put on paper what they have in mind, because it is not strong enough. Their thoughts are volatile, with no power.

04. Mentality of stagnation

One of the manifestations I've seen in people over time, is the following: when there is a change in their lives, in most cases, people have the perception that change is negative and start to think about everything worse. Then, they develop their mentality of stagnation; specifically the following idea appears in their minds: to be at least as it was before! Thus, they manipulate themselves by fear, and that fear is programming their subconscious. It is no accident that the most powerful tool for negative manipulation of people was, is and will be fear. Sure, fear is good because it keeps you in the safe zone, it will keep you alive, but when it seizes your mind, it becomes extremely harmful and paralyzes your mental forces.

05. Your Life Equation

The results you get in life are determined by a 5-step process:

- Step 1: Predominant thoughts;
- Step 2: Beliefs;
- Step 3: Decisions;
- Step 4: Continuous action;
- Step 5: Result.

Here is how it works:

Your predominant thoughts form your beliefs. Psychology and NLP are very clear in this regard. Further, beliefs are what determine your decisions. Put more simply: the strongest thoughts in your mind determine your decisions. Decision-making is the beginning of your life. Then, decisions are those that push you to action, and the action continues to determine your outcome.

Therefore, the result is in complete harmony with those predominant thoughts that govern your mind. So, what you get in life does not come by chance, but is the result of a 5-step process:

Predominant thoughts – Beliefs – Decisions – Action – Result

This process is extremely important to understand and integrate into your life, precisely because it makes you aware of the following fact: what you attract in your life is determined by the way you think. So, not the external environment determines your results in life, but your mental prevalent settings. The exterior is just the framework of your life game where you run and depending on how good you are in this game, you get a certain set of results. Therefore, some have fabulous results, while others live from one day to another.

Everything that gets a shape in the physical plane must first get a clear shape in your mind, then by concrete action, that shape in your mind materializes in the physical world. Therefore, the fairest indicator of how well you play the game of life is dictated by your results obtained correctly, according to the laws governing the Concept of Attraction. If you do not add the spiritual power to the creative process, your results will only be temporary, as you will rise and you will fall and again and you will rise and you will fall.

So look closely at the results of your life! They represent the most accurate indicator of how good you are. I know most people will say:
"Yes, I know, I understand, but I am much better!"
Here is the error in their minds: they make confusion between their beliefs and reality. What these people see is just the reality of their minds, but the world in their minds is not the big world. Most people think the world in their minds is the big world. And then, they create confusion between their beliefs and reality.

But understand that your results are the most accurate indicator of the level you are at the moment.
"Can you become much better?"
Of course you can!
"Will you act very conscientiously in this regard?"
That depends on you!
As you can see, it comes back to you. You are the leading unknown in the equation of your life.

Most people live their lives with only small increases from year to year, so if you make a blueprint of your life, you will find that on a period of 5 or 10 years, their quality of life has not improved much. Their life is reduced to how to pay their bills, how to solve problems that are increasing more and more, how to live from day to day. Metaphorically, it is as if these people are trying to cover holes in a boat. By the time they cover the first holes, other holes are already formed elsewhere in the boat. These holes are problems that they draw in their lives.

Most people revolve around problems. And as they spin longer, they have more problems. And then their life becomes a struggle. These are the people who go through life at random. They make the same set of actions that most people and therefore have the same direction as the majority and about the same set of results.

If this way of life is pleasing you, then it really is okay, but if your mind does not accept the way of life of the common man, then you need to improve your mental filters responsible for quality results. Allow me to remind you: Predominant thoughts – Beliefs – Decisions – Action – Result. Developing a new set of mental filters will bring a different set of results to your life. Similarly, changing the filters will change your mind and your life results.

06. Results by three different levels of labor

Now comes the important part related to work: there are three different levels of work by which you can get results.

- Level 1: Untargeted Work

This work creates extremely high physical and mental wear. Most people fall into this trap, they struggle to get where they want, sometimes they may even succeed, but they get exhausted because their work involves a lot of wear, much reaction to what is happening around, and a lot of inner struggle.

The result that you get by untargeted work is determined by two factors:

- daily workload;
- continuity (specifically, for how long).

At this level, you often force things to happen. This is the level where most people work. It is the lowest level that attracts results obtained by the most. For most people, prosperity means more work. Double prosperity means double work. This is their reasoning of their mind. Those who fall into this category do not have a long-term strategy. In the best case, they just set their desires in the future, but behind these desires there is no strong strategy with concrete action.

Untargeted work is the level of action happening without first putting your thoughts in order. If you do not put your thoughts in order, then no matter how much you work, it does not compensate for misalignment of your thoughts with the action you do. You are simply doing random work. Anything that appears in your way you think is an opportunity, the work you do is not directed to a clear purpose in the future. You simply work just to earn some money to live from one month to the next. You work hard to live hard. Next, I make available to you a simple test with only 4 questions, to see if you belong to this level of work, or to the next level, specifically the directed work.

Here are the four questions:

Question 1: Where do you plan to be in 5 years?

Question 2: Do you have an action plan with clear objectives that you follow?

Question 3: Look at your written plan. What % have you achieved so far?

Question 4: If you continue to work on your plan with the same speed you currently work, over 5 years will you record a big leap of results?

Read once again these questions, because they represent a real indicator of the direction in which you are going.

If you like the direction, I congratulate you. If you don't like it, you can change it even from today, and in a few years your results will be completely different and you'll have a clear direction in life.

- Level 2: Directed Work

The most important aspects of directed work are:
- experience that you have;
- the strategy behind the action.

Directed work is based on a powerful strategy and an action plan with concrete steps. Here you have to develop three levels of vision:
- short-term vision (1-2 years);
- mid-term vision (3-5 years);
- long-term vision (5-10 years).

At this level, you have the mental image of what you will become in the future and take continuous action in this regard, following a clear strategy and a well-organized plan. Directed work is a level where you feel the alignment of your conscious thoughts with the subconscious thoughts, specifically, that your inner beliefs align with what you want. Alignment is not at the maximum, but gives you a route to long-term results.

- Level 3: Inspired Work

Few manage to work at this level, since they must first pass the first two levels. You cannot work directly on level 3, because this is a process. This is the level at which the connection to the spiritual plane is stronger.

Peculiarities that define inspired work are two:

- spiritual power that you attach to your work (in this sense, the Concept of Attraction is an absolutely phenomenal instrument);

- synchronicities.

Synchronicities refer to those events, people, opportunities that arise in your life at the right moment, even if their likelihood was very low. Perhaps such synchronicities happened in your life. At this level, synchronicities occur often and are an indicator that you are on the right track. Basically, at this level, the road "*is shown to you.*" These synchronicities are like road signs announcing that you're on the right path. Inspired work is the level at which alignment of the conscious thoughts with the unconscious thoughts is complete, you feel inspired and the way is shown, live an "*in-spired*" life meaning "*in spirit*".

I know that most will likely say:
"Okay, from now on I will work at the third level."
But I recommend to you not to do this from the beginning, because you will not succeed.

Here is how it works:
- to work on the second level, first you have to understand very well the first level from a practical perspective;
- to get to the third level, you first need to understand the second level very well and from a practical perspective.

Moving from one level to the next is not achieved overnight. It requires a radical change both of your mental settings (i.e. the inner reality) and of your external actions.

Moving from one level to the next, in most situations, involves years of continuous personal development.

And you'll probably say:
"That long?"
However, the reality is that time will pass anyway, whether you do something towards results or not!
So I highly recommend to you to answer one question:
"What do you do with the time and skills you have available?"
Over 5 or 10 years, do you choose to stay at the same level that you are now or decide to work on a completely different level? What is your decision?
Here is a lesson to remember all your life: if you have not established a clear intention for today, you return to your yesterday's routine! Similarly, if you do not clearly establish what you want in the future and do not take concrete action in this regard, you actually live in the past.

07. Your Model of the World

Reality cannot be truly known. My reality and your reality are two different realities. This is why people have different perceptions and different beliefs. So we cannot talk about reality, but reality of your mind or my mind, which is actually a model of reality, but not the reality itself. I have my model of reality, just as you have your own model of reality. Is my model better than yours or rather is your model is better than mine? The answer is "No!" A model is not good or bad, but simply a model. Important is the effect it produces in your life. So, what you're really interested in, is the result obtained using the model and not the model itself.

Perhaps you wonder why I say this. The reason has to do exactly with the way we perceive reality: when you understand that each has its own model of the world, the tendency to see the world from a critical perspective disappears and you'll understand that who contradicts you, in fact has nothing to do with you. What he/she does is that he/she presents his/her own model compared to yours, and where models do not overlap, there are contradictions.

Therefore, those who enter into conflicting discussions with you, actually have nothing against you. They react because they feel that their model of reality is violated at a level of beliefs. Therefore, the other person is just trying to defend its own reality, since the person cannot escape his/her own model instantly to transfer to another model. It is a process of change, and this process leads on to expansion of the model.

So, here is the question:
"Do you believe in what I just said?"
If you do not, it means that there are beliefs in your mind that are opposed to what I say. But if what I just said has meaning and power for you, this happens because in your mind there are beliefs that validate what I said.

I'll give you a very simple tool for identifying your level of understanding the world. It is true both for you and me. There are three identification levels and I recommend that you identify the level where you are now, so you can go in the future to the next level. It matters less what level you are now, what is important is where you decide to go.

Are you ready? Let's start:

Level 1 (lowest): small minds gossip about other people;
Level 2 (the middle): average minds discuss events;
Level 3 (uppermost): great minds discuss ideas and concepts.

> *"Great minds discuss ideas,
> average minds discuss events,
> small minds discuss people."*
> Anna Eleanor Roosevelt

So what are you talking about: about people, events or ideas? Do not ignore what you read because you become what you think most of the time. Identify the level where you are and decide to think at the third level.

08. Act and the way will be revealed to you

In the materialization process, most people consume their time trying to see from the beginning how they will achieve the result. For example, if you have decided to make EUR 200,000, do not block yourself on the way in which you make this money. Do work related to you: develop your mind, adjust your attitude, identify your dreams and motivation, understand and apply the principles that govern success and build your plan of action to follow. Then you will get other better ideas, and then you'll make the necessary adjustments to the original plan. The nice part is this process will amplify more and more to the stage where you can identify ways to get that money more easily. Thus, you have drawn towards you the ways to get the object of your desire. You asked, you worked, you got it.

Many people actually remain stuck trying to see clearly from the beginning ways to get that money. And because it's hard to have the picture from the beginning, they enter into a state of deadlock and develop their conviction that the objective cannot be achieved. Thus, they lose confidence in themselves, and when they see others that have achieved results, feel inferior and develop their conviction that those around them are the best, smartest, coolest (Devalued Thought patterns).

The truth is that those who have achieved results applied faster the principles that govern success, even if at first it was not clear how to do it correctly. So no matter where you are now, you can get in your future much more than you have now. And the good news is that you have enough potential to do so, and thus, you don't have to be smarter than most, but the consistency with which you will apply the principles of success must be much more than that of most people. Remember that in life it matters less how low a problem gets you down, but makes all the difference how high it propels you and in which direction.

09. The power of change is within you

I know that most people have an erroneous thinking in the process of achieving prosperity. They think their chances are too small if they have little money to begin with and the chances of succeeding are only on the side of those who have money. But here is the reality: those who have less money are forced by circumstances to use their creativity, energy, time, skills, motivation, dream, attitude, more than those who have more money, while those who have more money will try to rely on that money for a change. In most cases, those with less money will succeed, because their resources for changing are interior and the change is driven mostly by internal resources.

10. What is the result?

No one else is culpable of the results of your life! You're responsible.
You can convince yourself of this fact, if you can answer the following question:

"What do the results mean?"
You might find this question strange. Maybe even feel a tend to answer in seconds. And I challenge you: Before reading further, give yourself the answer to the question:

"What do the results mean?"
This question deals with ignorance and then ignorance is transferred into your life.

So go back:
"What do the results mean?"
You're no better than your results or lack of results can show.

Perhaps you will say:
"Yes, BUT it is not so, because I actually can do more, I am actually better, I know more."
"No! No! No! You are exactly at the level that results in your life can show. Everything outside of results, at best, can be your potential."
When you say:
"Yes, BUT it is not so, because I actually can do more, I am actually better, I know more," actually what you're trying to do is just put the potential you possess in the spotlight.

However, the potential is different from result. It can be converted to results, only by action. This implies action plan, strategy, attitude, perseverance, communication skills, etc. The transition from potential to actual results is not easy. If it were easy, then everyone's result would be according to the potential they have. It's like having a car with 300 horsepower, but you cannot use more than 100 horsepower.

The result not only refers to what you get at the end of a work process. The result refers to the process itself, specifically, what you get is a result of a way of thinking and action over a period of time. Therefore, the term RESULT has a double meaning. And this is extremely important to understand.

Most people fall into the following trap: they undervalue the process itself, but this is actually what leads to the final result, i.e. to what you want to get. When you understand this mechanism correctly and integrate it into your life, you cannot blame external factors anymore. I'm not saying that there are no external factors that influence your results. Of course there are, but those factors actually were attracted by you, and should have as little influence as possible on your mind. If the external factors are stronger than your dreams, then the problem is you. This means that you deliberately allow the exterior to take possession of your mind, your thoughts and therefore on the results of your life.

PART 2: PRACTICAL INSTRUMENT FOR LAW APPLICATION

Even though I gave you practically a series of 10 tools of paramount importance in the implementation of this law, I will generously make available to you right now the correct strategy of setting targets and dreams. It is an eight-step strategy. So let's start:

Step 1: Set your Dream in Positive and Written form.

Defining your dream crystallizes thinking in a clear direction, so that your physical, emotional, intellectual energies are oriented towards this direction. The dream should be put in a positive form, not negative as most people do. If you set it in a negative form, your mind will see what you do not want and will actually materialize physically more of what you do not want.

A sample of objective in a negative form: I decided to get rid of poverty.

A sample objective in a positive form: I decided to get involved physically, emotionally and intellectually to achieve my dreams.

Step 2: Establish clearly the benefits you get if you realize your dream.

If your mind does not see the benefits, you will not find reasons strong enough to do the work. And then you stop. Without motivation, you start but you will stop shortly.

Step 3: Establish an Action plan (but in an ephemeral form).

Initially, you start with an action plan that you realize at the moment in the best shape you can. However, if on the route, you identify better solutions, then change targets, because after all what interests you is not the target, but the result. The central idea is that when you change targets actually go for the better, higher, faster, the direction is ascending. Makes sense?

Step 4: Check if you are willing to pay the price.

If you're not willing to pay the price of change (as it will be work, sacrifices, sleepless nights), then set your dreams at lower levels that your mind can accept. Jump to actions that are within the acceptance boundaries of your mind.

Adventure to bigger dreams only if you're willing to take greater risks. There are four prices that you will have to pay: physical, emotional, intellectual and financial.

Step 5: Set a deadline (the deadline can be changed later, but do not make a habit of it).

When you set a deadline, you actually establish a system of coercion for your subconscious. Otherwise, you will work towards your dream but you know when: tomorrow, after tomorrow, a week later, when it's hot outside, when there will be better times, when the children will grow up. In other words, you defer taking action again and again, since you have not set a psychic system of coercion.

Step 6: Follow the progress of results.

It is not enough just to do an act, to evolve you have to evaluate (what you did, where did you get, what do you do and how you can improve your strategy).

Step 7: Surround yourself with people who motivate you and help you realize your dream.

Find people around you who have succeeded, associate yourself mentally and emotionally with their way of thinking and action. Don't search for those who have failed in life, as this decision will lead you exactly in their footsteps.

Step 8: Be consistent – work daily towards your dream.

It is a concrete, continuous and large-scale action to a well-defined objective. Continuous action refers to action day after day, not just when you enjoy it.

And now, in the end of this law, this is what I want to tell you:

The greatest thief of dreams is right within you, and

if you let him beat you, your confidence drops to a level of mediocrity, where you will not be able to dream. The truth is that most people die at 25, but are buried much later, after 60 years! This is the image of people deprived of dreams, because a life without dreams is dead! In life, if you do not live your dream, then you live your nightmare! I want this statement to represent the emotional imprint of your mind.

PART 3: SUMMARY

Here is what the Law of the Organized Plan states: to get what you want, you have to work in this direction. I didn't say just to work, but I said to work in this direction. We're talking about directed, focused on results work, following a strong strategy and a well-organized plan, as untargeted work involves wasting your life!

The most important aspects of this law are:

01. What is your dream?
02. The direction of your future.
03. Think on paper.
04. Mentality of stagnation.
05. The equation of your life.
06. Results by three different levels of work.
07. Your model of the world.
08. Act and the way will be revealed to you.
09. The power of change is within you.
10. What is the result?

PART III. HOW TO MINIMIZE THE PAYMENT OF YOUR SPIRITUAL BILLS

SECTION 1: IDENTIFY THE SPIRITUAL MESSAGES

Next, I will help you understand the importance of identifying signals that you receive about events that are to materialize in your life (both pleasant and unpleasant). When you understand the mechanism by which you are notified, when you manage to decrypt the messages that are sent, well, that's a pretty big chance to control the course of events at a certain level. Of course you cannot control all events, because this is not possible, but you can alter the course of events that could change your life in a radical way.

In this regard, I will tell you two real cases to understand the mechanism of interpretation behind actions. For privacy reasons, I will not provide personal data of those involved in the events.

I will help you understand on some level, how you can decrypt the messages you receive about major events that will materialize in your life physically. When you understand the meaning of messages, you can change the course of events and thus minimize the payment of your spiritual bills. Remember the change of any event or outcome in your life starts with awareness. Then, through concrete action, you can change the outcome.

In conclusion, you can change the course of events in your life to a certain level, when you understand the meaning of messages you receive and jump to concrete action to change the vibration of those events.

CASE 1:

The course of events

This case concerns a young 34-year old man who was in a car accident, resulting in extremely serious physical and emotional trauma. Now he is paralyzed, can barely move his hands, and he will have to spend his entire life in a wheelchair. He has a plate where he has lost a part of his skull and another plate that supports his spine.

Seven months before this painful event, he was left by his wife, and he sees the daughter he had during the marriage increasingly less, since his ex-wife does not want him to meet their child unless she receives an amount of money. This situation has generated recently more emotional imbalances. Currently, the only help he receives is from a younger sister who feeds him and helps him to move.

Here is how the accident was materialized: carried by the emotional imprint of the events in his life, one Sunday he decided to go to a party, to which he was invited. However, on this road he attracted the accident that destroyed all his life.

Interestingly, a year ago in the same area and around the same time in the fall, on a weekend day, he was involved in another accident in which the car was almost entirely damaged. Following the event, he had just a few injuries, but he acquired a very strong fear. But this time, the car was partially damaged, and he suffered the accident that put him forever in a wheelchair.

As an emotional calming mechanism, this young man who was paralyzed, decided to associate the painful event with a life lesson trying to discover what God wanted to send to him. From the desire to understand the message behind the events that occurred in his life, he realized that he was in fact informed of what would happen, a year ago. At the first event, although he received the signal that is in the vibration of accident, practically he understood almost nothing, and had not decrypted or translated the message.

Here is a brief dialogue with him:
"Tell me please, how had your life changed after this accident?"

"I was stupid, I did not understand anything in my life until now and I had not realized how beautiful the moments I should have lived were. I had many women, I hurt them, I tormented them, and now I cannot even see my baby."

"I became a scoundrel, who is 34 years old, helpless in a wheelchair. All I can do is wait for the day to pass as quickly as possible and then go to sleep until somewhere, sometime, my life will end."

What must you understand from this case?

We, as human receptors, can get a notice in space and time coordinates, that we are close to a "*spiritual bill*". Spiritual bills must be paid in some form. When you have bills for payment, you must pay them as soon as possible, in order to settle them. The fact that a person has an accident is not a coincidence, since the accident is really just the result, a manifestation in the physical plane of spiritual payments.

Think about it: if the young man would have been delayed just a second, then he wouldn't have been in that time and space and so the event would not have occurred. A simple trivial conversation would have slowed him and he could have avoided the accident. But his spiritual bills were ready for payment and a message was sent one year before the accident, but he did not understand it, and payment was painful. Nobody wants, at the age of 34 to end his life as a parent and as a man, and this image is simply devastating.

- What should he have done in that period of one year so as to stop or lessen the physical materialization of that accident?

The first step would have been to identify signals from the moment they began to manifest.

- How do you identify these signals?

Here is the answer: you are involved in accidents from which you escape relatively easily, hear more and more people talking about accidents, increasingly think of accidents, become receptive to news about accidents, meet people who speak or have been involved in accidents, practically put on your mental screen the image of accidents and thus you create the circumstances to materialize them in the physical plane.

So, he should have become responsive to the signals received from the outside and set in his mind those images that were in fact at the polar opposite of the signals received. For example, if he received as signal an accident which he escaped easily, he had to place permanently in his mind the following emotional thoughts: every time I drive, I have a quiet road and attract only pleasant events and smiling people.

The problem is that, ordinary people do not understand what is going on in their lives. In general, they are far from understanding these aspects, far from controlling their thoughts and feelings, even less able to decode them and try to seek solutions for them. The average man does not understand that an accident from which he escaped is just a signal that says a spiritual bill is coming, he does not understand that the accident may be repetitive and somewhere in the future may even destroy his life, as it was the case of this young 34-year old man.

Although he was informed, he did not clean the vibrations of the accident at the energetic level, he had not changed anything in his consciousness, he used the same mental programs and practically he created the conditions to materialize the accident.

Everything that happens to us in the physical world first appears in the energetic field. There are in fact three levels of manifestation: spiritual – energetic – physical.

The spiritual plane is the source of all manifestations. After the spiritual plane, the energetic level is reached, and after the energetic plane, the physical manifestation occurs.

In other words, materialization in the physical plane is just the end-result. Until then, the person is informed, receives signals and has the responsibility to identify them.

Here is what I want to tell you: you are solely responsible for all events that occur in your life. Through your emotional thoughts, you generate conditions to materialize the events in your life.

So, control your thinking and you will control the vibration in which you are constantly, and this vibration will attract into your life people, circumstances and opportunities that correspond to the vibrations you generate.

It is therefore essential to understand that you will not physically attract what you want, but you will attract what is inside you, by the sum of all vibrations that dominate your mind. The main reason for which people draw in their lives all kinds of random events is illustrated by the fact that their minds were defocused, full of random thoughts. In this situation, they do not channel their physical, emotional, intellectual energy towards a clear direction that would lead to concrete results. And afterwards, they think they cannot. And when they think they cannot, then they really cannot. To be as effective for you, I will detail this process about the human potential in the second section of this chapter.

CASE 2

The course of events

I was the prisoner of my own life where the bars I was leaning were heavy sufferings that followed me for over 40 years. I had a life of suffering, year after year. I have 36 years of experience as a teacher, but my professional identity says little about my painful life when I really wanted my death. And for that, I thank God, because from this heavy and continuous pain, a new life was born.

After a childhood in which I was influenced by alcohol, traumatized by the swearing and beating in my family, two marriages with physical and mental abuse followed, so at the age of 30 I had reached rock bottom in my life. Amid the stress and negative thinking, devoid of love and understanding, attacked by an aberrant panic, I ended up in the psychiatric ward, knocked down by chronic fatigue and depression. Absence of the husband from home, lack of money and daily cares overwhelmed me so much that for a period of four years I made two suicide attempts. I took over a hundred antidepressants once to escape the ordeal, after which I placed in a hospital, in coma for five days.

People around me left me. I went through two traumatic divorces, but this pain helped me to know the power of God.

From all the pain I felt and I gathered into myself so many years, a burning desire for change was born. I felt how I become dependent on this need of transformation on a daily basis. I did not see the slightest glimmer of hope, but inside me, I felt strongly that my life will follow a different path. My desperate attempts to find a solution to take my life out of this nightmare, led me to a man. I did not know him and I did not know anything about him.

He trained my mind, helped me to change my attitude, my thoughts, to apply the Law of Attraction in my life, taught me how to be always in a state of joy and inner motivation that would attract the things I want. He helped me build a big dream, and made me accountable to achieve it. I clung desperately to this dream, I firmly believed in it, I felt that is the chance of my life to leave such a painful and dark past. I advanced and overcame many challenges step by step.

In January 2013, I was spiritually richer, full of life, and hope was alive in me. I had a big dream, I knew what I wanted to do with my life! I knew who I was and I believed in the value I had! A desire to change my life was burning in me. I worked with a lot of consciousness, and I began to achieve goal after goal. My desire for change was so strong that in four months I managed to publish a book. When I started writing this book, I only had a folder with blank sheets. But after six weeks I finished the manuscript and I stopped. I got a publishing house to publish my book but I had no money.

But I worked with Law of Attraction as my coach taught me. I was confident that I would succeed, and soon information began to flow about publishing houses and the money I needed so much to print the book came as well. For me, it was a miracle. I felt God help me. Thus, on December 11, 2013, five months away from when I started writing the book, I saw another dream come true: launching my own book. I enormously enjoyed the results of my work and I understood how the Law of Attraction works.

In 2013, for several months, I viewed airplanes and tickets, I felt very strongly that I will go somewhere. In November 2013, my brother with whom I was talking quite rarely, called me from Milano and told me: "I bought a ticket and I expect you here for the holidays." I had never left the country before. Another dream was fulfilled. "Thank you!" I felt miracles happening in my life.

Now I have an enlightened mind, I smile and I am happy, I feel like a kid who enjoys life and beauty. I am grateful for the changes in my life and I am thankful each morning that I live and I have a special mission. I thank my coach, Gabriel Radu (author of this book).

What must you understand from this case?

For a more accurate interpretation that creates an overview of this case, I will analyze it both psychologically and in terms of how the Concept of Attraction manifested in her life.

For nearly 40 years, she has attracted negative events that came to her one after another. It was basically a process of chain reactions that began in her childhood, when she had no control over events. This traumatic period of her life, positioned her in predominantly low-frequency emotional states, which placed itself in her psycho-energetic system and constituted a process triggering chain reactions. Basically, this was the period in which the conditions that would attract increasingly traumatic future events were generated.

From a psychological point of view, there were two possible directions of mental and physical activity:

01. To accelerate the chain of events in the process of materialization until the mind and body crack and physical death occurs;

02. To cling desperately to a powerful dream and put into that dream a passion that defies logic.

The psychological mechanism that made possible such a great change was determined by two critical factors:

01. on the one hand was the pain accumulated over time;
02. on the other hand was a burning desire for change.

In this case, the expression of the Law of Attraction can be observed both during the chain of negative events materialized and during the time when she clung desperately to a powerful dream that set it in her mind, then down to her heart and worked with a lot of consciousness to give life to it. Basically, she could have decreased the payment of the spiritual bills if she was understanding long ago the functioning of the Concept of Attraction and the process by which she drew negative chain events.

In achieving this dream, she used the painful past, which she released in her book. She had no money and no publisher to publish her book, but had confidence that she will succeed. She had no experience in writing, but had great pain and great desire for change. What the emotional mind thought, became reality. Her strong faith and reality aligned and become one. And that works for her, for me and for you. We all obey the same universal laws.

The power of change is within you. You just have to use it correctly. When you position yourself with faith in the vibration of what you want, you'll attract people and circumstances that you need to give life to the dream that lives in you.

SECTION 2: IS THE WALL TOO HIGH?

When evil and negativity are manifesting deeply in people's lives, they have a habit of blaming anything but themselves. They blame the others, the system in which they live, work peers, the government, parents, misfortune and even karma. They believe that life is unfair.

I know it's hard to accept that you are solely responsible for your results, especially when you are very low, because in your mind, the problem is not you. It is anywhere else, but not you. And then, you feel problems as a very high wall that you cannot jump over. You will not say it's your fault, but you say that the wall is too high.

But you know what? Actually the problem is just you, because it is not the wall, but you are not good enough to jump the wall. Those who have passed the wall, managed, but not because of luck. They succeeded because of their skills. When you lack skills, you'll say the wall is too high. And so, you start to get connected and to sympathize with those specific beliefs of people who failed to pass the wall. You will hear stories and you'll find yourself in them. And then you'll accept them as a reality of your mind. I challenge you! Listen to their stories. They will plead excuses, and the reason of their failure will be outside of them. But the reality is that excuses do not make people better or smarter.

On the other hand, listen to the people who made it. You will find that they do not rely on excuses. They could do that, but they do not. They talk about the right attitude that helped them, the dream that helped them to raise, the challenges they had to overcome.

Basically, you will find two kinds of people situated mentally and emotionally to polar opposites, who had to pass almost the same walls. Some succeeded, others found excuses for not succeeding! They both invoke what governs their minds. Why do I say that? Because I want you to think very hard what are the walls of your life that keep you captive. No matter how hard you work, until you put your mind in order, you will fail to overcome those walls since they are only in your mind, not physical. Those are the beliefs that keep you glued on the spot, they are the demons of your mind that you brought to life and developed increasingly stronger, finding all sorts of excuses for the injustices of your life.

So let me ask you:
"How long from now, will you decide to give power to those demons inside of you?"
"How long will you decide to stay trapped between walls?"

In the end, for your sake, I challenge you! Take a sheet of paper and a pen, draw a vertical line in the middle of the sheet. To the left of the sheet write the minus sign and the plus sign to the right. If this book has brought value to your life, then do one more last crucial step for the results of your life. Under the minus sign, write the worst three things that can happen if you build your future after these fundamental laws governing a life of wealth and success.

Under the plus sign, write the best three things that can happen if you follow the laws I revealed to you in this book.

Now rip the sheet in half along the line drawn. What you need to do next is significant for your mind as it is related to the decision you will make regarding your future. Here is what to do: choose one of the two halves of paper and keep it with you permanently, read it daily with as much emotional involvement as possible, until you feel that what you have written on the sheet is manifesting in your life. Set the other half on fire. Do not throw away, but physically and mentally set it on fire. Then focus your whole attention day after day, on the other sheet.

Focusing your attention in a clear direction means to get involved only in the direction of those objectives that lead you to a large-scale continuous evolution. The other actions have no power to change.

Maybe you are afraid to take action! And I ask you:
"Do you think you lack the courage to change the results of your life?"

If you do not lack courage, it means that you are in the process of change! Congratulations! But if you're not in the process of change, this means that you lack courage, you are afraid to take action.

But if this is the truth of your mind, then let me ask you:
"What does courage mean to you?"
Come on, think very seriously about the answer before reading further.

*"Courage means being afraid
to do something, but still doing it."*
Knute Rockne

YOU ARE THE CREATOR OF YOUR OWN DESTINY AS TODAY'S THOUGHT WILL BECOME THE REALITY OF TOMORROW!

Gabriel Radu

THANK YOU FOR READING THIS BOOK!

BIBLIOGRAPHY

01. Arntz, William., Chasse, Betsy., Vicente, Mark. *What the Bleep Do We Know?!*, Carte Daath Publishing House, Bucharest, 2007.

02. Braden, Gregg. *The Divine Matrix: Bridging Time, Space, Miracles, and Belief*, Publisher: Hay House, 2008.

03. Byrne, Rhonda. *The Secret*. Adevar Divin Publishing House, Brasov, 2007.

04. Byrne, Rhonda. *The Secret*. Adevar Divin Publishing House, Brasov, 2011.

05. Cayce, Edgar. *Soul and Spirit*, Divin Publishing House, Brasov, 2009.

06. Hicks, Esther and Jerry. *Law of Attraction.* Teachings of Abraham, Prestige Publishing House, 2007.

07. Proctor, Bob. *Attract money into your life*, Audiosfera Publishing House, Bucharest, 2008.

08. Proctor, Bob. *You were born rich*, Adevar Divin Publishing House, Brasov, 2009.

09. Sevigny, Daniel. *Secret key*, Nicol Publishing House, Bucharest, 2010.

10. Tracy, Brian. *The future depends on you: 12 key factors of the unlimited success*, Curtea Veche Publishing House, 2004.

11. Vitale, Joe. The Key. *The secret to attract everything you want*. Meteor Press Publishing House, 2009.

ABOUT THE AUTHOR

Radu Gabriel is a (life & business) coach, motivational teacher, author and entrepreneur. He is the founder of Programarea Succesului, a brand of personal and professional development, built around the slogan: "YOUR success is programmable".

His programs are a mix of professional techniques in the following fields: Concept of Attraction, Coaching, Leadership, Success Strategy Programming, NLP, Advanced Communication, Motivation.

His mission is to respond in terms of objectives and concrete results, to all those who made the decision to really improve the quality of their lives.

More details on:
www.programarea-succesului.ro

www.ingramcontent.com/pod-product-compliance
Lightning Source LLC
Chambersburg PA
CBHW031349040426
42444CB00005B/237